D1086840

ON THE ROAD
TO CHRISTIAN UNITY

An Appraisal of the Ecumenical Movement

ON THE ROAD
TO CHRISTIAN UNITY

An Appraisal of the Ecumenical Movement

BY SAMUEL McCREA CAVERT

Harper & Brothers · Publishers
New York

TO TWILA

"Teacher, tender comrade, wife,
A fellow-farer true through life"
and a constant co-worker
in ecumenical interests

CONTENTS

PREFACE

From the standpoint of overcoming the age-old divisiveness in the church, the last fifty years have been the richest in Christian history. In the pages that follow, I try to appraise the experience of the five decades, discover where it leaves us today, examine some of the major problems of tomorrow, and discern the goal toward which we move.

During almost all of this half century, it has been my privilege to have firsthand contacts with the movement for Christian unity. I am therefore tempted to approach the subject in terms of the personalities with whom I have been associated and to indulge in reminiscences of them. I resist the temptation—with occasional lapses! The subject itself is vastly more important than any of the figures connected with it. As Harry Emerson Fosdick remarks in his autobiography, "a man need not be in himself very great to be used by a great idea." In the case of the ecumenical movement, the idea at the heart of it is so resplendent that personalities fall into the background.

In *A History of the Ecumenical Movement*, edited by Ruth Rouse and Stephen C. Neill, we have an admirable chronicle of developments from the period of the Reformation down to the establishment of the World Council of Churches in 1948. There is no need at this time for another record of the historical events. What I present is less a factual narrative than an evaluation. Two reasons impel me to undertake the appraisal. One is the need for a careful analysis of the complex factors in the ecumenical picture in order to understand better where we now are. The other is the urgency for looking frankly at the troublous issues which the

9

World Council of Churches will be confronting in the years ahead.

These issues include difficult internal problems, such as the attitude of the Protestant and the Eastern Orthodox bodies to each other and the relation of the Younger Churches of Asia, Africa, and Latin America to the older churches of the West.

There are still more perplexing issues that concern the external relations of the churches of the World Council with Christians outside its membership. Among these are substantial bodies of Protestants, some having the most conservative backgrounds, others belonging to newer groups like the Pentecostals. Even more puzzling is the role of the Roman Catholic Church, which is beginning to show a surprising interest in the ecumenical movement.

Finally, it is important to shed as much light as possible not only on the stage just ahead but on the more distant goal. More particularly, we must try to get a sound perspective on the divergent views of those who regard enlarging co-operation among the denominations as the essential genius of the ecumenical movement and of those who see its true destiny in the union of the separated bodies in one visible Church. There is at present a great uncertainty at this point. How the uncertainty is to be resolved is the major long-range question.

To some readers it may seem that I am more preoccupied with matters of organization than with the inner spirit. It is true that I am constantly asking how our unity in Christ is to be corporately expressed and made manifest to the world. But I am always conscious of the fact that the ecumenical movement, in its ultimate meaning, is not ecclesiastical structure. It is people—people in the world-wide Christian fellowship, people bound together in Christian love, people trying to reflect their common relation to Jesus Christ in their relation to one another.

That is why I use the term "Christian unity" in the title although strict precision in language might require me to speak of "church unity" instead. Christian unity refers to a community of thought, feeling, attitude, and conduct. Church unity has more explicit reference to institutional forms and relationships. I am concerned with both. Even though it is the latter which I discuss most, I employ the term "Christian unity" for the purpose of accenting the qualities of spirit that must underlie any significant unity of structure—whether in the form of federation or of union.

To other readers, it may seem confusing that sometimes I speak of "the church" and at other times of "the churches," although referring to the same entity. In what sense are we justified in calling our present welter of diverse Christian bodies "the church"? The answer to this question is the book as a whole. But at the outset we may remind ourselves that all "the churches" are part of a reality greater than themselves. They all belong to an ecumenical Christian community, which we call "the church," even though it has no adequate embodiment in recognizable form.

The central thrust of this book is to indicate why and how "the churches" are becoming more truly "the church." This is intimated by the phrase, "on the road," in the title. "On the road" suggests movement and the forward look. The greatest obstacle to a unity beyond our present denominational system is our persistent inclination to look backward—to Thomas Aquinas, to Luther, to Calvin, to Wesley, or to some other point of reference in the past. This tends to make us think in static terms. If we are to have a more ample unity, no group of Christians may regard itself as having arrived—it must know that it is always "on the road." We all need to recover the New Testament conception of Christians as the Pilgrim People of God. A Pilgrim People are not permitted to settle down comfortably at any stage. They must think of themselves as "not having received what was promised, but having seen it and greeted it from afar" (Heb. 11:13). For those who see the Christian community in these terms, renewal and reformation are always insistent principles of its life.

Four of the chapters of this book, the first two and the last two, were given in a briefer form as the William Henry Hoover Lectures under the auspices of the Disciples Divinity House, Chicago, November 17–20, 1958. I am grateful that the responsibility of giving these lectures forced me to engage in more intensive and reflective thinking about problems with which I had been busily concerned on the practical and administrative side for forty years.

Since this is less a historical chronicle than an interpretation, less a record of objective facts than of personal judgments about them, footnotes and documentary references are not extensive. The Selected Bibliography, however, includes a reading list for each chapter, calling attention to the publications which have been most helpful to me.

For many insights that have entered into this appraisal, I am indebted to a host of colleagues. Their manifold contributions to both my experience and my thought have given me a deeper appreciation of the truth of John Donne's oft-quoted remark that "no man is an island, entire of itself." To single out any of the many to whom I owe so much is almost invidious. But to two, now in the Church Triumphant, I pay a special tribute: William Adams Brown, my teacher in Union Theological Seminary, who was most responsible for my early interest in the ecumenical movement, and William Temple, Archbishop of Canterbury, who embodied my highest ideal of ecumenical leadership.

I appreciate the courtesy of Bethany Press and the Pulpit Digest Publishing Company in permitting me to use a few paragraphs that have appeared in slightly different form, in *Christian Unity in North America: A Symposium* (St. Louis, 1958) and in editorials in *Pulpit Digest*.

SAMUEL McCREA CAVERT

New York
1961

ON THE ROAD
TO CHRISTIAN UNITY

An Appraisal of the Ecumenical Movement

Chapter I

THE ROAD WE HAVE TRAVELED

Survey of a Half Century

As recently as the beginning of the twentieth century, there was nowhere in the world a permanent organization of churches for co-operation on a national or international scale. Anyone who is not past middle age can hardly realize in what disconnected compartments the churches then lived. Although Christian men and women might work together across denominational lines, the churches as corporate bodies went their separate ways.

During the last half century, three different roads have been traveled which have converged to form the ecumenical movement of today. Their signposts designated them as co-operation in missions, co-operation in Christian life and work, and co-operation in problems of faith and order. Each of these three approaches led through a distinctive terrain of its own. At the outset, none of them was broad enough for more than a meager traffic. Their coming together has resulted in a highway of spacious proportions.

The traffic on the three routes got under way at approximately the same time. In 1910, the World Missionary Conference in Edinburgh signaled the development of official co-operation in missions on an international basis. Later in the same year came the initial proposal for a World Conference on Faith and Order. Two years earlier, in 1908, the Federal Council of the Churches of Christ in America, a major factor in co-operation in Christian life and work, had come into being. This eve of the First World War was a period of unprecedented fruitage of impulses toward Christian unity.

In society at large, this was a time of heightened awareness of the oneness of our world. The dimensions of the earth were shrinking to those of a single neighborhood. The oceans that once separated peoples had become connecting channels of international trade and communication. The Wright brothers' airplane had got off the ground at Kitty Hawk in 1903. The first radio microphone had been installed in 1908. The automobile had emerged from its experimental stage with the production of the Model T Ford in 1909.

The mood of the era was so hopeful that a religious journal had hailed the coming of the twentieth century by changing its name to the *Christian Century*. A hymn written in the year before the Edinburgh missionary conference rejoiced that "the day of dawning brotherhood breaks on our eager eyes." What was not anticipated was that the new means of drawing mankind together might be used for ends more divisive and demonic than the world had ever known.

The Missionary Road

The missionary movement of the nineteenth century had carried the Christian gospel to all the important nations of the earth and had made the church for the first time a world-wide community. "Edinburgh 1910" was a great symbol that the church had begun to recognize itself as a global fellowship. As nothing else had yet done, it dramatized international co-operation in fulfilling the world mission of the church.

There had been, of course, considerable missionary co-opera-A full century earlier, William Carey had even proposed a "gen-tion, although sporadic, long before the Edinburgh conference. eral association of all denominations of Christians from the four quarters of the world" which would meet decennially to consider common problems in missionary work.[1] Although this idea was quickly dismissed as "one of Brother Carey's pleasing dreams," there were consultations from time to time during the subsequent decades in several centers of Asia and in London and New York. The Edinburgh conference, however, was epoch-making in two respects. First, its delegates came not merely as individuals interested in missions but as representatives officially appointed by missionary societies. Second, it created an international executive body, modestly called a Continuation Committee, with a budget and a secretariat for carrying on the work which the conference had begun.

This Continuation Committee was the first permanent interdenominational organization of international character and scope. To us today, the formation of nothing more than a Continuation Committee of a conference may seem to have been a small and cautious step. So it was, if judged in the light of developments since 1910. But it marked the beginning of a new ecumenical era.[2]

The Edinburgh missionary conference marked the end of an era as well as the beginning of one. The old era, whose passing was not yet discerned in 1910, conceived missions as a movement from "Christendom" as a "home base" out to a "non-Christian world." Christendom and the non-Christian world were then thought of as entities that could be described in geographical and cultural terms. Christendom was identified with the civilization of the West. The non-Christian world was in Asia and Africa. To-

[1] Ruth Rouse, "William Carey's 'Pleasing Dream,'" *International Review of Missions*, Vol. XXXVIII (1949), pp. 186–192.

[2] Informative reminiscences of the Edinburgh missionary conference by the man who was its executive secretary are given by J. H. Oldham in "Reflections on Edinburgh 1910," *Religion in Life*, Summer 1960, pp. 329–338. For a full account and interpretation both of the conference and of what resulted from it, see W. Richey Hogg, *Ecumenical Foundations* (New York: Harper & Brothers, 1952). Both Oldham and Hogg emphasize a strategic aspect often overlooked—the participation of the Anglo-Catholic missionary organization, the Society for the Propagation of the Gospel. This set a precedent which has been significant in the subsequent course of the ecumenical movement.

day, the picture of the Christian mission as rooted in the West and from there projected into the rest of the earth is obsolete. There are two reasons. One is that we now see that there is no such thing as Christendom defined as a geographical reality. The other is that in Asia and Africa there are now Christian churches which, although still small, are sharing with the churches of Europe and North America in a missionary responsibility.[3]

Four years after the Edinburgh missionary conference, the most terrible war that mankind had known burst upon the world. This so greatly multiplied the obstacles to international co-operation among the churches that it was more than a decade before the Continuation Committee could develop into a constitutional structure. In 1921, however, the International Missionary Council emerged, through which missionary agencies of the West and new national Christian councils in Asia, Africa, and Latin America were brought together for continuous consultation and planning. The Continuation Committee, even though it had no official standing in the churches as a representative body, under the vigorous leadership of John R. Mott and J. H. Oldham had laid necessary ecumenical foundations by bringing a network of national Christian councils into being.

THE "LIFE AND WORK" ROAD

While the missionary enterprise was thus creating its pattern of international co-operation, another road in the direction of Christian unity, commonly known as that of Life and Work, was being explored. On a national scale, its course had been indicated prior to the Edinburgh missionary conference. The date which most clearly reveals this development is 1908, when the Federal Council of the Churches of Christ in America came into being. This was the first official and corporate avowal by any large group of separated churches anywhere in the world that they had so much in common by reason of their relation to one Lord that they would

---

[3] This thought is well developed by Lesslie Newbigin in *One Body, One Gospel, One World* (London and New York: International Missionary Council, 1960), pp. 27–29.

come together and stay together in a common witness and a common service.

The Federal Council represented a rising concern in American Christianity for the kind of practical unity which could be attained through co-operation in spite of all the differences in doctrinal and ecclesiastical matters. Its constitution, drafted in 1905 and ratified by thirty denominations between 1905 and 1908, boldly declared that the time had come "more fully to manifest the essential oneness of the Christian Churches of America in Jesus Christ as their Divine Lord and Savior" and declared its first objective to be "to express the fellowship and catholic unity of the Christian Church."

Although the Federal Council was, in principle, related to all of the interests of the member churches, the thrust of its program during its early years was strongly on the side of Christian social responsibility. A new social consciousness had been coming to birth. Leaders in the churches were awaking to the challenge of social and industrial conditions. Their concern, however, was not widely appreciated among the rank and file of church members. Peter Ainslie, a prophetic spirit among the Disciples of Christ, even records that when he began to attend the early meetings of the Council he did not tell his Baltimore congregation lest his participation be regarded as grounds for firing him!

The emphasis on social responsibility led to sharp attacks on the Federal Council throughout the forty-two years of its life—as also upon its successor, the National Council of the Churches of Christ in the U.S.A. One type of attack came from groups within the churches that clung to an exclusively pietistic tradition and could not see that the church had any other function than the conversion and nurture of individual souls. A second type of attack came from the extreme right wing of political and economic conservatism that resisted any social change. The support of the Council during its early years was so frail that it barely survived. Dean Shailer Matthews records that when he was invited in 1912 to become its second president, he hesitated to accept because it looked as if the Federal Council were already moribund.

Those whose memories do not reach back for a half century often assume that the Edinburgh missionary conference was the fountainhead of the entire ecumenical movement. This is a grave oversimplification of the historical events. It was, indeed, the first of the great international Christian assemblies, and its influence on subsequent world-wide co-operation was creative in the highest degree. But it was the experience of the American churches with the conciliar principle that provided the pattern of organization which was followed in the creation of the World Council of Churches.[4]

The American contribution was channeled directly into the ecumenical traffic through the Universal Christian Conference on Life and Work held in Stockholm in 1925. The concern with social problems was, of course, not limited to the American churches. In Great Britain, it came to an interdenominational climax in a Conference on Christian Politics, Economics, and Citizenship in 1924. But it was on the continent of Europe, surprisingly, that the most dynamic leadership of the Life and Work movement appeared. This was in the person of Archbishop Nathan Söderblom, primate of the Church of Sweden. He had agonized over the impotence of the churches to prevent or mitigate the horror of the First World War. He saw in this an indication of the tragic weakness of the churches as a force for shaping the ethical standards of the world.

In many lands, there proved to be sufficient sentiment of this character to make possible the first international conference devoted to the objective which Stockholm set for itself: "to unite the different Churches in common practical work, to furnish the Christian conscience with an organ of expression, and to insist that the principles of the Gospel be applied to the solution of contemporary social and international problems."[5]

In addition to bringing the social responsibility of the churches

[4] On this point, see William Adams Brown, *Toward a United Church* (New York: Charles Scribner's Sons, 1946), pp. 45–52.

[5] G. K. A. Bell (ed.), *The Stockholm Conference, 1925.* (London: Oxford University Press, 1926), p. i. Bell, then Dean of Canterbury and later Bishop of Chichester, was the secretary of the conference.

to ecumenical expression, the Stockholm conference marked an advance in two other important respects. For one thing, it represented the action not of specialized agencies but of churches as corporate bodies. Although much of the preparatory work was done by the World Alliance for International Friendship through the Churches, an organization of prophetic individuals which had then been in existence for a decade, most of the delegates were at Stockholm because of decisions made by denominations officially. They represented not groups with a specific interest but the churches as organized in their total life.

A second aspect of the Stockholm gathering that was pregnant for the future was the presence of representatives of Eastern Orthodoxy. This was the initial occasion when that historic branch of Christianity participated officially in one of the great, modern ecumenical conferences. This new relationship meant that Eastern Christianity was emerging from a thousand years of isolation from the West. Stockholm established the principle that the ecumenical movement was to be much more than a pan-Protestant affair. An Orthodox participant, Archbishop Germanos, was to be—twenty-three years later—one of the presiding officers at the first Assembly of the World Council of Churches.

THE "FAITH AND ORDER" ROAD

At Edinburgh, it was agreed that the goal of carrying the gospel to the world could best be achieved by concentrating on this common purpose and excluding doctrinal and ecclesiastical differences from consideration. At Stockholm, it was similarly assumed that the way to get ahead in practical tasks in relation to society was to work together without worrying about issues which separated the churches. In both cases, it was felt that realistic objectives would be blocked if theological divergencies were brought into the picture.

There were some, however, notably Bishop Charles H. Brent, who felt that the differences could not be thus bypassed. He had been at Edinburgh in 1910 because of his missionary responsibility in the Philippine Islands. He was alert to the new demands for

Christian social witness as voiced at Stockholm. He was a strong
advocate of interchurch co-operation. But he felt it imperative to
go further and to call the continuing existence of the denominational system into question. The result was the exploration of a
third ecumenical road—in the realm of the doctrine and structure
of the church. At his instigation, the General Convention of the
Episcopal Church in 1910 proposed a World Conference on Faith
and Order. Seventeen years later, it met in Lausanne and launched
a sustained effort of the churches to understand each other at the
level of their sharpest ecclesiastical divisions.

At Lausanne in 1927, there was sufficient agreement in basic
theological conviction to enable the delegates to issue a unanimous
statement on "The Church's Message to the World." When, however, they came to the nature of the church, its ministry, and its
sacraments, there was a complete impasse. It became plain to all
that if a common mind were ever to be achieved on such stubborn
points as these, it would be only after a long and intensive process
of common study.[6]

The distinctive "plus" which the subsequent studies in Faith and
Order have brought into the ecumenical movement is a deeper
and wider sense throughout the churches of the wrongness of their
divided state. Fifty years ago, the divisions were generally accepted
as natural and inevitable. They were defended as necessary mani-
festations of Christian freedom and as representing the only pattern within which legitimate diversity could be maintained. Today, there is far less complacency with the situation. We do not
know how to overcome the divisions, but at least we see how far
our denominational system falls short of being an adequate fellowship of One People of God. As a result, a new relationship between
Christian scholars of different confessional traditions has come
about. Instead of merely entrenching themselves within their respective redoubts, they are collaborating with one another in trying to understand what contributions other traditions than their
own have to make to the Church Militant.

[6] For a full account see H. N. Bate (ed.), *Faith and Order: Lausanne,
1927* (London, SCM Press, 1927).

For more than twenty-five years, these three interests—co-operation in the missionary task, co-operation in Christian life and work, and co-operation in studying issues of faith and order—pursued their independent ways. They were all expressions of a quest for greater unity, but they had their origins in different centers of concern and moved along parallel and unconnected paths.

The separateness of the three paths, however, could not permanently continue. Those who were following them had too much in common to be indifferent to one another. Within each movement, there were those who thought of it only as a functional organization for achieving their own specific objectives, but others envisioned a broader goal. Concerned for the whole life of the whole Church, they saw that the three movements belonged together. Among those who most clearly held this synoptic view was William Adams Brown. Earlier and more persistently than any other leader, he began to press for the union of Life and Work with Faith and Order.[7] Active in both, he was convinced that each was an essential complement of the other. While in England in 1933, he suggested to the Archbishop of York, William Temple, then chairman of the Continuation Committee of Faith and Order, that there be an unhurried conversation among a few representatives of the main ecumenical agencies. At the invitation of the Archbishop, ten persons (of whom I had the privilege of being one) came together at his home in York in May of that year. The only immediate outcome was an agreement that the members of the group would keep in close touch with one another, but the little meeting marked a turning point. Thereafter, it was not the independence of the agencies but their togetherness that received the accent.

In 1937, a definite converging of the separate paths began. As the

[7] As evidence that my judgment about Brown's contribution is not too much colored by long friendship with him, I quote a comment made in a personal letter by J. H. Oldham, who was the organizing genius of both the Edinburgh, 1910, and the Oxford, 1937, conferences: "I entirely agree with you that the coming into existence of the World Council of Churches was due to the vision and persistence of William Adams Brown more than to the effort of any other man."

result of a consultation of thirty-five leaders in the Life and Work and Faith and Order movements just prior to their second conferences, held in Oxford and Edinburgh respectively, a plan was projected for uniting the two movements in a new, comprehensive structure as the World Council of Churches.

ENTER THE WORLD COUNCIL

When the thirty-five consultants came together at Westfield College in London in July, 1937, no one quite expected so far-reaching an outcome as a proposal for a world-wide council of churches under a constitutional government. This outcome was made possible by a rich experience of ecumenical fellowship and collaboration during the two decades preceding. Even when some form of unification had been agreed upon by the conferees, it was felt by several that the names of the two organizations should be preserved, perhaps by some such clumsy designation as Joint Commission on Life and Work and Faith and Order. When Archbishop Temple, as chairman of a subcommittee on recommendations, finally asked, "What name shall we now give the child?" I timidly suggested, "How about World Council of Churches?" After a brief silence, the Archbishop remarked: "Why not? That's what we really need and want." So "World Council of Churches" it came to be.

Both the Oxford Conference on Life and Work and the Edinburgh Conference on Faith and Order approved the recommendations in the following month, although at the latter the Bishop of Gloucester voiced grave misgiving over the creation of an ecclesiastical body which might become involved in controversial public issues such as were dealt with in Life and Work.

At Utrecht in May, 1938, a Provisional Committee for the World Council of Churches in Process of Formation, created in accordance with the decisions of Oxford and Edinburgh, drafted a constitution—with the counsel of a larger advisory body—and submitted it to the churches of the world for their consideration. The outbreak of the Second World War the next year delayed the convening of the first Assembly of the Council for a decade, but at last it met in Amsterdam, on August 22, 1948, representing one hundred forty-six churches in forty-four countries that had approved the constitution.

The Amsterdam Assembly was unquestionably the most widely representative gathering of the churches that had ever been held. In both geographical and denominational comprehensiveness, it marked the highest ecumenical peak that had been seen up to that time. The delegates came from member churches in every continent and from the major countries of the world, with the exception that from the Communist area the churches of only two countries—Czechoslovakia and Poland—were represented.

At this stage, the International Missionary Council was not included in the plan for uniting the ecumenical agencies. It had a strong organizational structure, based on national Christian councils and national missionary conferences rather than directly on churches. It had had the longest experience of any of the agencies in international work. It warmly supported the proposal for a World Council of Churches, but felt it sound policy to maintain its separate existence for a time as a body concentrating exclusively on missionary responsibilities.

Shortly after the constitution of the World Council had been drafted, a joint committee representing the World Council in Process of Formation and the International Missionary Council was appointed as a means of mutual reinforcement. After the World Council had come into formal existence in 1948, the two bodies were officially defined as "in association" with each other. This association was so vital that a plan for full integration was drafted eight years later. Under this plan, the International Missionary Council becomes the World Council's Division of World Mission and Evangelism. As soon as this union is officially ratified, the converging of the three ecumenical roads into one broad highway becomes complete.

In the process by which the three movements have drawn together, the weightiest influence has been their inherent need for one another. At the Stockholm conference on Life and Work, it had become obvious that differences in the realm of social attitudes and policies often reflected deep-rooted differences in theology—for example, in the understanding of the biblical concept of the Kingdom of God. At the Lausanne conference on Faith and Order, it appeared that some of the obstacles to unity were as sociological as theological—for example, in the class divisions of society. And both Life and Work and Faith and Order, if they were really to be world-wide movements and not merely Western, found themselves inextricably involved with the missionary movement and the Younger Churches that were related to the International Missionary Council.

Another influence that made the three movements more ready to become integrated in a council of churches was the growing recognition of the significance of the church as a corporate community in our modern world. This was greatly stimulated by the rise of secular totalitarianism, which, in the form of both national socialism and Communism, threatened the entire Christian tradition. This made all thoughtful Christians more aware of the need for an organizational strategy in which the church as church would stand out clearly before the world as a community with its own distinctive character and ethos.

The New Ecumenical Dimension

So the ecumenical movement began to be conceived as something more than the sum of the existing international organizations. It meant more than co-operation in important tasks. Its function was (in the words of W. A. Visser 't Hooft) nothing less than "to demonstrate the true nature of the Church in its oneness, its universality, its apostolic and prophetic witness in the world."[8] This role the ecumenical movement could not fill if it were itself parceled out into three separate parts. The unity and wholeness of the church had to be made more visible to the world.

The wartime decade between 1938 and 1948, while the World Council was still in process of formation, was a time of painful ordeal. It is a marvel that the feeble structure could survive all the

[8] Ruth Rouse and Stephen C. Neill (eds.), *A History of the Ecumenical Movement* (Philadelphia: Westminster Press, 1954), p. 701.

strains of the conflict, when direct contacts among the leaders of the churches in warring countries were almost entirely cut off by political barricades. But by functioning in three parts—one in Geneva, one in London, and one in New York—the Provisional Committee was able to hold together. In fact, the tie actually became stronger and more precious. At a time when the world was split asunder in its political and economic life, there were many for whom the sense of a spiritual oneness in the Christian community became intensified.

German Christians like Martin Niemöller, Johannes Lilje, and Dietrich Bonhöffer might be in prison, but they were not excluded from a conscious fellowship with Christians in England and France and America. Bishop Eivind Berggrav might be held incommunicado in Norway, but he inspired ecumenically minded Christians everywhere. The little staff of the Provisional Committee in Geneva—including a Dutchman, a German, a Frenchman, a Swede, and an Estonian—held the movement together at the center, kept an amazing number of contacts with key persons in the warring nations, and in their own relations with each other were the nucleus of an ecumenical family.

A concrete incident will serve as an illustration of the way in which channels were kept open in spite of the war. When the American Federal Council decided in 1942 to send a messenger to Geneva for consultation, it fell to me to undertake the trip, an intricate journey by way of Portugal, Spain, and southern France. The joy of the Geneva friends at seeing a representative of the American churches after a separation of three years was moving in the extreme. It was on this occasion that the first tentative memorandum was drafted setting forth the prospective need for postwar reconstruction and relief in Europe. This memorandum, which I took back to America only a fortnight before the Nazi occupation of southern France made further personal contact with Geneva impossible, was the basis for the preliminary steps in forming what is now the Division of Inter-Church Aid and Service to Refugees in the World Council.

A remarkable feature of the drawing together of the churches in the ecumenical movement of the last five decades is that it has taken place during the very time when the world in its political life has been falling apart. It was the period in which there were two world wars, the most internecine in all the centuries. It was likewise the period of a long-continued "cold war" between the Communist and the free areas, with the world divided into two nuclear-armed camps.

One of the most creative aspects of the development has been the interplay of influence between American Christianity and European Christianity as they have come into living touch with each other in a two-way traffic. To comprehend this is to discover that the ecumenical movement is no mere co-ordination of static institutions but a potent force of mutual stimulus and renewed vitality.

What America Gave and Received

In the perspective of a half century, we can now discern what the American churches have given to the ecumenical movement and what they have received from it. Their special contribution seems to me to have been at two main points. In the first place, they brought to the common store the most successful experience in co-operation to be found in any country in the world. In the second place, they contributed a lively concern for making Christianity relevant to the life of society in our own time.

On the other side of the ledger, the American churches have received from the ecumenical movement two highly significant lessons. For one thing, they have gained a new dimension of theological depth, corrective of their own pragmatic temper. For a second thing, they have acquired a deepened appreciation of the place of the church in the Christian experience and have become more church-centered in outlook.

Let us analyze, somewhat more concretely, how this mutuality of influence has made itself felt.

In their concern for Christian unity, the American churches have manifested a far stronger interest in a practical approach than in the theological method characteristic of European Christianity. Their emphasis has been on working together to achieve certain definite results, rather than on discussing doctrinal and ecclesiastical differences arising from divergent interpretations of the Bible and from diverse historical backgrounds.

This is true in spite of the fact that the Faith and Order movement had its origin in America. Although there were outstanding American Christians who were deeply committed to the search for agreement in the realm of the doctrine and the order of the church, the dominant mood was one of impatience with such an approach. It seemed too "theoretical." Co-operation in the areas of practical agreement was accepted as a sound and sensible way of moving ahead toward unity, without waiting for some far-off possibility of a united church based on a common statement of faith and a common ecclesiastical polity. The American attitude might have been expressed in John Drinkwater's "A Prayer":

> Knowledge we ask not,—knowledge Thou hast lent,
> But, Lord, the will,—there lies our bitter need;
> Give us to build above the deep intent
> The deed, the deed.[9]

The bustling activity of American Christians—with their enthusiasm for projects and programs, organizations and budgets—was sometimes a source of irritation and even of amusement to European Christians. According to a little joke which they liked to tell, three Americans were caught in an airplane accident and had to bail out in their parachutes. Before they reached the ground, so the story goes, they had organized into an association and had elected a president, an executive secretary, and a treasurer!

The activistic temper of the churches doubtless reflected the spirit of the American nation as a whole. The emphasis on experiment and decision and responsibility had been characteristic of a people in a new world where there was a virgin continent to be occupied, where there were challenging difficulties to be over-

[9] *Poems 1902–1919.* Copyright 1919 by John Drinkwater, published by Houghton, Mifflin Company, Boston, and used by permission of Curtis Brown, Ltd. and the author's estate.

come, and beckoning opportunities to be embraced. As was said by Frederick John Turner, the interpreter of the historical significance of the American frontier, the ever expanding movement westward encouraged a "practical inventive turn of mind, quick to find expedients."

While this approach to problems of the churches often led to superficial procedures, we can be grateful for the spirit of determination which was not content merely to discuss an issue, but insisted on doing something about it. We may also rejoice that the experiment of American Christians in working together at concrete tasks in councils of churches provided the general pattern which has been found valid both for other lands and for the ecumenical movement as a whole.

Along with their experience in co-operation, the American churches brought to the ecumenical movement a special emphasis on Christian social responsibility. Here, too, their accent was pragmatic. They were generally regarded by Europeans as lacking in theological concern. "American activism" was a frequent term of depreciation among the theologians of Germany and other Continental countries in the period following the First World War. In self-defense, Americans sometimes reproached their European colleagues—and not without justification—for carrying on theological discussions in a purely theoretical framework, detached from the social context and the social needs of the time. In practice, what happened in this new confrontation of American and European Christianity was a cross-fertilization which has proved fruitful on both sides and has been one of the most creative aspects of the ecumenical movement.[10]

THEOLOGY AND SOCIAL ETHICS

The European criticism that the American social emphasis lacked theological depth had considerable validity. A review of

[10] For a well-documented treatment of this development, to which I am greatly indebted, see Paul A. Carter, *The Decline and Revival of the Social Gospel* (Ithaca: Cornell University Press, 1954), chaps. 8, 9. See also, as a more popular treatment, Ronald E. Osborn, *The Spirit of American Christianity* (New York: Harper & Brothers, 1958), chaps. 1, 4.

the pronouncements either of the Federal Council or of its member churches during the three decades prior to the Second World War will show that many of them were expressions of a general humanitarian concern more than interpretations of the Christian gospel in its own distinctive import for society. What the pronouncements set forth was highly commendable, but often not very different from what was being said by secular idealists and reformers.

Evidence of this is found in the remarkable document known as "The Social Ideals of the Churches." Formulated by the General Conference of the Methodist Episcopal Church in 1908 and given interdenominational sanction at the first meeting of the Federal Council later in the same year, it was a historic landmark. It was the sign and symbol of the new social conscience that had been gathering momentum in American Christianity. It takes a stretching of the imagination for us today to realize how unprecedented it then was for a national group of delegated representatives of major churches to make such an affirmation as that they stood for the right of workers to organize. But the statement of ideals, while owing much to a heightened appreciation of the moral passion of the Hebrew prophets and of Jesus, lacked a firm and explicit foundation in the distinctive Christian understanding of the nature of God and man and society.

Even though there was little explicit theological formulation, a true theological insight was implicit in the concern for problems of society—an insight into the Lordship of Jesus Christ over the whole of man's life. This underlying conviction had a firm grip on those who were at the center of the Federal Council's work. It was involved in the constitutional declaration that one of its objectives was "to promote the application of the law of Christ in every relation of human life." It found expression in Frank Mason North's memorable hymn, which the Council constantly used:

> Where cross the crowded ways of life,
> Where sound the cries of race and clan,
> Above the noise of selfish strife
> We hear Thy voice, O Son of Man.

Whatever the theological inadequacy of the so-called Social Gospel, it succeeded in focusing Christian attention on contemporary social conditions and the social responsibility of the churches. Two or three incidents from the Federal Council's history will suffice as concrete illustrations. At a time, for example, when the twelve-hour day, and even the seven-day week, were still regarded as an unavoidable aspect of the steel industry, the Federal Council invited the National Catholic Welfare Conference and the Central Conference of American Rabbis to join it in a study of the situation. The study coincided with such a rising public concern that a few weeks after the issuance of the report in 1923, the largest steel company announced its abandonment of the twelve-hour shift. Behind the study lay an inquiry into the steel strike of 1919 by the Interchurch World Movement—a short-lived organization which is now remembered only for this one notable action. A special reason for the influence of the study was that the co-operation of Protestant, Roman Catholic, and Jewish representatives in the 1923 report was the most striking example of interfaith collaboration that the nation had seen.

From the Council's inception, four large Negro denominations were included in its membership on an equal basis. In 1921, a permanent commission on race relations was established. As early as 1924, a quadrennial meeting of the Council was held in Atlanta, Georgia, with no segregation in seating arrangements in the church in which it was held—the first time that this had happened in a public gathering in the city.[11] In international affairs, the best illustration of the Council's role was the work of the Commission on a Just and Durable Peace during and after the Second World War. The study conferences on the relation of the churches to world order gave a potent voice to the Christian conviction that there should be a permanent structure for international co-operation. The Commission was the first body with a large national constituency to make its support of an organization like the United Nations widely heard.

[11] This was made possible chiefly by the bold initiative of John J. Eagan of Atlanta, first chairman of the Federal Council's Commission.

The shortcomings of the Social Gospel movement in its earlier stage were chiefly owing to its relative neglect of the theological foundations. A realistic biblical theology would have provided a needed correction of its too romantic optimism and would have been a reminder of the stubborn fact of sin as something to be reckoned with in every generation and in every form of human society. This more realistic note which later came into the American outlook was largely the result of contacts with European churchmen. The gulf between the two points of view was widest in the years immediately following the First World War, and came conspicuously into the open at the Stockholm conference on Life and Work in 1925. By the time of the second Life and Work conference, held in Oxford a dozen years later, a *rapprochement* between the two viewpoints was appearing. In the process of ecumenical conversation, a new outlook emerged on both sides. American churchmen discovered that their social enthusiasm needed more theological perspective. European churchmen learned that their theological formulations, abstracted from contemporary social life and experience, lacked the relevance that gives them vitality.

Rediscovery of the Church

Another important result of the engagement of American and European Christians with each other in the ecumenical give-and-take was that the Americans gained a deeper sense of the centrality of the church. In the early phases of the Social Gospel movement, in spite of its concern with society, there had been slight recognition of the significance of the church as itself a society of its own unique kind. The distinction between the church and the world was blurred. It would hardly be too much to say that in their commendable eagerness to come into effective contact with the secular environment, the American churches had been in danger of becoming secularized themselves. To guard against such an outcome, a clear and firm doctrine of the church was essential. This shortcoming was remedied by participation in the ecumenical movement.

The growing interest in Faith and Order was helpful at this point, for one of its initial and persistent concerns has been the nature of the church. Another influence in the same direction was the enlarging contacts with the Younger Churches of Asia and Africa. As minorities in Buddhist and Hindu and Moslem environments, they needed a Christianity embodied in a recognizable community, not merely a vague religious atmosphere.

It was the Oxford conference on Life and Work in 1937, however, focused on "Church, Community, and State," which was most important in giving American Christians a deepened appreciation of the church. After Oxford, the Social Gospel began to have a new orientation. The church now came to be viewed not as an instrument for social welfare and the reform of secular society, but as a God-given community, transcending divisions of nation, race, and class, and providing visible evidence of what God means society as a whole to be. Probably the strongest influence of Oxford upon American Christianity was to make it more church-centered.

The exhortation "Let the church be the church!" which was often heard at Oxford was sometimes misunderstood as advocating a withdrawal from secular affairs and a retreat into ecclesiastical and institutional interests. Its real thrust, however, was in exactly the opposite direction. It was a way of insisting that the church must have its own essential ethos as a precondition of exerting its rightful influence on society at large. If the church is to count significantly for international unity, for example, let it be the church, truly a world-wide Christian fellowship, not an arm of a national state. If, again, the church is to affect the traditional pattern of racial segregation, let it be the church, a truly interracial community whose standards are derived not from its environment but from the gospel.

The strategic importance of the church as a community of its own distinctive kind, owing final allegiance to Christ alone, is reinforced by a perceptive appraisal of the present crisis in our cultural situation. We used to take it for granted that Christianity and our Western civilization were in sufficient rapport to justify the expectation that society would be increasingly molded by Christian ideals. Today, we have to assume the existence of tension between them, rather than harmony. The tension can be observed in a dazzling clarity in an area like East Germany, where the church is fighting a constant battle with a Communist regime to maintain its own characteristic life as a Christian community. A similar tension, although in a more latent and subtle form, ought to be discerned in America, which is in the midst of a disturbing trend to identify Christianity with American culture. There is ample reason to wonder whether the popular upsurge of religion is as much a matter of Christian conviction as of conformism to what is regarded as an acceptable social standard.

In the face of such a conformist trend, nothing is of more crucial import than a community of faith and worship and life which has a historic rootage not dependent on any contemporary culture, a community which knows itself to be grounded in the ultimate nature of our human existence, a community which has no national or racial limitations but is as universal as the love of God in Christ. Such a community is the Christian Church as the ecumenical movement now sees it.

The deepening appreciation of the church was reflected in the establishment of the National Council of the Churches of Christ in the U.S.A. in 1950. This marked a new stage in co-operative unity. It rested on the insight that all the functions of the church are so interdependent that they ought to be integrally related to one another. As the movement of co-operation had gained momentum, it had expressed itself in an increasing number of organizational forms—more than a dozen national structures. In addition to the Federal Council, there were interdenominational agencies representing boards and societies with specialized interests like foreign missions, home missions, Christian education, and stewardship. Although each separate instrument was playing its own part well, the total effect was far from orchestral. The formation of the National Council meant a recognition that all the agencies belonged together in a symphonic whole as instruments of one Christian community.

The fact that the many different interdenominational agencies were finally able to unite in a National Council and submerge their separate identities within it is encouraging evidence that ecclesiastical institutions do not have to be sunk in well-worn ruts. Each of them might easily have said, "We have a praiseworthy heritage and are rendering commendable service: why not go on in the old way?" The reason they did not say this was because their primary loyalty was to the church rather than to a particular interest or organization. They had been captured by the vision of the church as "the whole body, joined and knit together by every joint with which it is supplied" (Eph. 4:16).

From this survey of the last half century it appears, in summary, that there have been three great awakenings within the churches, all on a world-wide scale: (1) an awakening to their common responsibility for a world mission; (2) an awakening to their common responsibility for the character of human society and culture; (3) an awakening to the wrongness of their divided state and to the spiritual necessity for a truer manifestation of what it means to be the Body of Christ in the world.

These three awakenings and the growing sense of their being inseparable aspects of one ecumenical movement have produced the World Council of Churches as we know it today. The whole development has taken place during my own generation. What has happened was so unpredictable fifty years ago that no interpretation of it can be adequate which does not conclude that the Holy Spirit is at work in a contemporary renewal of the church.

Chapter II

THE CROSSROADS WHERE WE ARE

Survey of the Present Scene

After fifty years of ecumenical journeying, we should be able to get a realistic perspective on our present situation. How far have we actually come? Along with advances have there been slowdowns and setbacks? Like Alice in Wonderland you feel you ought to "get to somewhere . . . if you ran very fast . . . as we've been doing." But it might be true, as the Queen rejoined, that "it takes all the running you can do, to keep in the same place."

Although we have reached no Wonderland of unity, we are certainly not in "the same place" as a half century ago. The most decisive gain is that we now have the essential structures for interchurch co-operation in common responsibilities. Fifty years ago a council of churches of any kind was a novel experiment. Today it is a familiar part of the religious landscape—local, national, and international.

In the United States, there are more than nine hundred councils in cities, counties, and states, created by the churches and directly responsible to them. The National Council of the Churches of Christ in the U.S.A., made up of thirty-four denominations and functioning in the whole range of their interests, not only is firmly rooted in the ecclesiastical soil but has substantial influence in American life. There are also national councils of churches, or national Christian councils, in most of the other major countries or regions of the world. Climaxing the development in co-operation is a World Council of Churches, with a membership of one hundred and seventy-eight churches, including Eastern Orthodox and Old Catholic as well as Anglican and Protestant, in fifty-three countries.

A Structure for World-Wide Co-operation

The diversities comprehended within the World Council of Churches indicate how remarkable an achievement in unity it is. It includes Christians of all the continents and all racial backgrounds. It embraces churches on both sides of the dividing line between Communist and free societies. It takes in bodies as ancient as the Patriarchates of Jerusalem and Antioch and as new as Bantu churches of Africa that became autonomous only yesterday. It is capacious enough to have room for a church as hierarchical as the Greek Orthodox or as informal in structure as the Society of Friends. Here is, beyond question, the most widely representative association of churches that the world has ever seen. One runs no risk of exaggeration in saying that there has been a highly impressive development of the organizational structures requisite for effective co-operation.

Along with the rise of the conciliar structure at local and national and international levels has come a rediscovery of the church as a unique and distinctive community. When I began my ministry nearly fifty years ago, most Protestants did not think of the church as integral to the redemptive purpose of God and to the Christian faith. They regarded it as an important institution which men had created for fostering religious and ethical interests. A typical illustration of this viewpoint was a ceremony prepared for rural churches. It made use of a large candle symbolizing Christ as the light of the world. Around it were clustered smaller candles which, after being lighted at the central flame, were placed all on the same level. One of these candles stood for the church.

Others represented the school, the Grange, the farm bureau, the home bureau, the Four-H Club, the Boy Scouts, and the town government. While the excellent intention was to suggest the Christian influence in all of life, the church was reduced to one good agency among others. There was no interpretation of the great biblical pictures of the church as the People of God, as the Body of Christ, as the Fellowship of the Holy Spirit.

The recapturing of the biblical understanding of the church is a main factor in the vitality of the ecumenical movement of today. It does not think of the church as merely an association of individuals coming together because of their common spiritual interests. Instead, the church is the People of God, called into a covenant with Him to be the instrument of His purpose for the world and sustained in the world by His providence. The church is not thought of as constituted simply by the action of men pursuing idealistic aims. It is divinely created to be the Body of Christ for carrying on His mission in history. The church of the ecumenical movement is not envisaged as a company of congenial and like-minded neighbors. It is the *koinonia* of the New Testament, in which the bond of fellowship is a common relation to a Living Lord and a common participation in His continuing life.

The extent to which the adjective "ecumenical" is now a part of our Christian vocabulary is evidence that something new has entered into our contemporary situation. The deepening sense of the Church Universal and of oneness among Christians of different historical traditions has made an over-all descriptive word necessary. Today we are all becoming accustomed to "ecumenical." The adjective is a way of affirming three closely related and freshly apprehended aspects of the church: first, its unity derived from its origin in one Lord; second, its world-wide character; third, its mission to witness to the lordship of Christ over the whole life of mankind.

It is important to note the difference between being *interdenominational* and being *ecumenical*. Although both involve cooperation, there are overtones of meaning that are characteristic of each. Interdenominational efforts do not in themselves raise any question about the validity of denominations as they now are. In the background of the ecumenical movement, however, is always an implication that the church is a single reality given to us by Jesus Christ in and with the gospel.

This ecumenical viewpoint subjects the denominational system to continuous self-criticism and never permits us to assume it is an adequate manifestation of the one Body of Christ. The increasing awareness of the contradiction between "the holy catholic Church" as an article of faith and the present fragmentation of Christianity in the world is a seminal aspect of the stage which we have now reached.

What the World Council Is Doing

Although the ecumenical movement is indelibly stamped with the conviction that it is of the very nature of the church of Christ to be an undivided whole, there is a long, long road to be traveled before the empirical churches reflect this truth. The existence of the World Council, however, is a pointer in that direction. The most important thing about the Council at the present stage is what it is rather than what it does. It stands as the great testimony that the churches are no longer satisfied with either national or denominational separateness. It indicates the highway along which they are together seeking an embodiment of their essential unity and universality.

While the most significant thing about the World Council is just that it exists, what it does is of far more than incidental moment. Although it has been in official existence for only a brief period, its activities are some of the most dynamic features of the Christianity of our time.

Consider, for example, its program of mutual helpfulness, reaching across both national and denominational lines, described as interchurch aid. Begun as an emergency project of postwar relief and reconstruction while the World Council was still in process of formation, it has met such a spontaneous response that it is now accepted by the churches as a normal part of their ongoing life. Of this service a careful scholar, Bishop Stephen C. Neill, even says that "in the whole history of the Christian Churches there has never been so great, so sustained, and so simply generous a manifestation of Christian charity."[1]

In the main, this channeling of fraternal help from church to church does not require extensive administrative operations by the Council. Its role is that of co-ordinator of efforts that would otherwise be sporadic and unrelated. Its chief function is that of an all-observing sentinel, alerting the churches to needs in any part of the world and enabling them to meet the needs under a concerted plan. If a disastrous flood or earthquake or other calamity strikes anywhere, the Council appeals to its member churches to share in the crisis. The program, however, is far more than dealing with emergencies. It is a continuous ministry of mutual reinforcement among churches that are equal in status but unequal in resources. Speaking in monetary terms, the total expenditure to which the World Council is thus related in at least a consultative way is in the neighborhood of ten million dollars a year.[2]

In one part of this program, that of service to refugees, far more than a co-ordinating role is assigned to the World Council. In this case, it is charged with an extensive administrative function in behalf of the member churches. This is for the obvious reason that the ministry to refugees, demanding constant contacts with many national governments and intergovernmental agencies, is the kind of operation which cannot be carried on at all without a large measure of centralized direction.

Judged by any standard, the service of the churches to refugees through the World Council is a magnificent achievement. Since the end of the Second World War, it has helped to resettle more stateless refugees and displaced persons than any other voluntary organization. It has a field staff of nearly five hundred workers in forty-six countries. Within a single year (1957), it found new homes for no fewer than 28,146 refugees. During the twelve years

[1] *Brothers of the Faith* (Nashville: Abingdon Press, 1960), p. 147.
[2] *Interchurch Aid in 1959:* A Report of the Division of Inter-Church Aid and Service to Refugees (Geneva: World Council of Churches, 1960), p. 26. In America, Church World Service functions as the arm of the Division.

since the World Council was formed, its record of persons reset-tled exceeds two hundred twenty-five thousand—an average of about fifteen hundred every month without a break. At the same time, it has ministered to far larger numbers of refugees who could not yet be moved from their camps or other places of asylum.

This service to refugees is not confined to those of the World Council's own household. The establishment of a colony of five hundred Russian "Old Believers" on a six-thousand-acre farm in Brazil after a long exile in Hong Kong is a conspicuous illustra-tion of this. Another is the effort in the Middle East in behalf of Arab refugees who are predominantly Moslem. The whole refugee program is one of pure humanitarian service in the name of Christ. It is visible proof that there is a spirit within the church which seeks not merely to further institutional ends but to minister to a world in need. It expresses the reality behind Baron von Hugel's remark: "Christianity has taught us to care. Caring is the greatest thing—caring matters most."

INTERCHURCH AID AS A FORM OF UNITY

More important than either the size or the immediate service-ableness of the program of interchurch aid is what it signifies. It is a real and recognizable form of Christian solidarity on a world-wide scale. It is a manifestation of what St. Paul was speaking of when he described the church as so much "one body" that "if one member suffers, all suffer together" (I Cor. 12:26). It represents the unity of love and mutual concern for which he set the pattern when he initiated an offering among the churches of Macedonia and Achaia for the relief of the church in Jerusalem (Rom. 15:15–27). These Gentile churches differed sharply from the Jerusalem church, especially at the point of the rights and obligations of Gentile Christians, but St. Paul knew that there was a common bond at a deeper level. The common bond was both demonstrated and strengthened by this first recorded instance of interchurch aid, and the same thing is true on a far vaster scale in interchurch aid today.

There are, of course, aspects of unity which interchurch aid does not touch, but at least it is a convincing reply to the prevalent misconception of the church as so divided that each sector cares only for its own denominational interests. Within the ecumenical circle it is no longer assumed, for example, that Methodists will help only Methodists, Anglicans help only Anglicans, and Disciples help only Disciples. There are too many cases not only of their helping one another but of their all helping the Eastern Orthodox who were once outside the realm of concern of any of them. To "bear one another's burdens" is an elemental feature of the oneness of the church, and in the World Council's interchurch aid this kind of unity has sufficient actuality to be, in some measure, visible to the world.

In the course of its development, interchurch aid has come to mean far more than physical relief. This tangible phase is, in fact, its lesser part. The greater thing is the strengthening of fellowship and mutuality in the world-wide Christian community. The program represents a new realization among separated Christians that they really belong to one body of Christ's people throughout the world. Large aspects both of Christian solidarity and of Christian statesmanship, quite apart from the financial, are involved.

For one thing, the moral and spiritual support of strong churches is being brought to weak minority churches struggling to maintain their witness under oppressive conditions. The Waldensians in Italy and the Evangelicals in Spain are cases in point. Their tie with Christians in other lands gives them encouragement, and reinforces their disadvantageous position in their own lands.

Again, two historic branches of Christendom—the Eastern Orthodox and the Protestant, isolated from each other for centuries—are being drawn closer to each other. The assurance of alert Protestant concern when the Ecumenical Patriarch was coming under heavy political pressure in Istanbul in 1955 is one of many examples of the changed situation.[3]

Another strategic phase of interchurch aid, psychological and spiritual rather than material, is the contact that is being main-

[3] See chap. 4 for an interpretative account of the role of Eastern Orthodoxy in the ecumenical movement.

tained with churches in the Communist orbit. In spite of all the political obstacles, the World Council has kept channels of communication open. This has prevented Christians in the Communist nations from being wholly insulated from fellow Christians in the free world and from the influences of world-wide Christianity. This is of the utmost long-range importance for the future of the churches under Communist regimes. It is also a needed demonstration that Christianity is not tied to any political or economic system, but transcends all patterns of human culture.

In a few of the Communist-dominated areas—Czechoslovakia, Hungary, Poland, East Germany—there are churches which are full members of the World Council. In 1956, it was even possible for a meeting of its Central Committee to be held in Hungary— an occasion made eventful by the reinstatement of the Lutheran bishop, Lajos Ordass, in the leadership of the church after having been forced out by the government eight years earlier.[4] As for the Church of Russia, although it rejected any relation with the World Council in 1948, it has now found a basis of tentative and informal contact through sending "observers" to meetings of the Council's Central Committee.[5]

Still another crucial aspect of interchurch aid, on both the material and the spiritual side, is the relationship of complete mutuality that is being established within the World Council between the churches of America and Europe on the one hand and the churches of Asia and Africa on the other. The history of missions has been so intertwined with the history of nineteenth-century colonialism that Asian and African Christians, whose nations are rapidly emerging from the colonial era, are understandably restive over a situation in which their relation with churches of the West continues to be mediated through a foreign-mission agency. This seems to them to imply a dependent and inferior status. They naturally want a church-to-church relationship on a plane of obvi-

---

[4] Unhappily, Bishop Ordass was later forced out again on charges of non-co-operation with the government.

[5] For a summary of relations with the Church of Russia in the years between 1948 and 1960, see pp. 82–84.

ous equality. The World Council of Churches has "come into the Kingdom for such a time as this," affording a new center in which East and West can share on the same basis in the world-wide Christian community.[6]

Interchurch aid, in broader connotations such as these, is not merely a program for meeting certain temporary problems. It is a manifestation of Christian unity, a revealing of what it means in spirit and practice for the church to be one Body of Christ. It is, of course, unity in only a partial and restricted form, but within these limits there is unity of a bona fide character.

UNITY THROUGH ECUMENICAL STUDY

If ecumenical aid is a preliminary form of unity, so also—although less obviously—is ecumenical study. As now developing, it is much more than a matter of research and survey. The program would be more accurately described as self-examination in an ecumenical setting. It is a process whereby Christians of different historical traditions and backgrounds engage together, on a world-wide scale, in a continuous probing of problems that vitally affect them all.

The idea that churches should promote serious study is, of course, not novel. What is novel is the provision for studying the same issues at the same time under a long-range common plan. This makes possible a growing consensus of Christian conviction around the world. The processes of study go far beyond the printed page and include consultations, conferences, and other forms of face-to-face meeting, all the way from small groups in local communities to national gatherings and international assemblies.

The projects of study are at the growing edges of the Christian mind of today. A major one has to do with the common Christian responsibility in areas of rapid social change, focused on those countries in Asia and Africa where revolutionary developments are proceeding apace, where peoples are awaking to a new sense

[6] See chap. 3 for a fuller treatment of the role of the Asian and African churches in the World Council.

of human rights and freedom, and where industrial societies are supplanting the simpler rural communities of the past. In most of these countries, the churches are so small that their attention has been concentrated on their own internal problems. The study of rapid social change is an effort to help them find ways of identifying themselves more fully with the fortunes of the people as a whole.

More oriented to the Western world is an intensive study of religious liberty and the relation of church and state, with the primary focus on the policies of Roman Catholicism. Among the salient aspects of the inquiry is the evidence of divergent trends within Roman Catholic thought today. The traditional position, defined in encyclicals of the nineteenth century, is that "error" can never claim the same rights as "truth" and that the Roman Catholic Church is therefore entitled to special privilege from the state. Over against this dominant view, the study cites influential voices within the Roman Catholic Church which are trying to bring its official position into accord with the principles of a pluralistic and democratic society.[7]

The most extensive and continuous line of ecumenical study is directed to the Faith and Order of the churches, and the barriers that now prevent full Christian fellowship. The inquiries in this field are chiefly theological, having to do with the different conceptions of the church, the ministry, and the sacraments. There is also a sociological side, concerned with social and cultural factors that conduce to separation and set up roadblocks to union.

There was, of course, an abundance of theological study before these ecumenical discussions of Faith and Order began. But in the main it was study designed to defend an established confessional position or to combat the position of others. It was parallel to the situation in the United Nations as described by Martin Buber when he once visited it. The exponent of the "I-Thou" relation said that "no one seemed to be speaking with any one else, no

---

[7] The full report, drafted by Carillo de Albornoz and documented with extensive citations from contemporary Roman Catholic sources, is published under the title *Roman Catholicism and Religious Liberty* (Geneva: World Council of Churches, 1959).

one was really listening to what another was saying, there was no real interchange or penetration." This comment about political debates could be transferred, point by point, to what was long the condition in theological argument. The present studies of Faith and Order are not of that type. They are open-minded conversations carried on by men of different schools of thought seeking to understand, and to learn from, one another.

The study program as a whole is a serious intellectual and educational undertaking but it is more than that. It is a necessary base for any significant progress toward unity. An effective strengthening of the organizational relations of the churches must have a firmer foundation in a common facing of common problems and responsibilities than now prevails. The unity we seek is not static but dynamic, and therefore calls for constant rethinking and renewal. What Socrates said about the individual is equally true of the church: "The unexamined life is not worth living."

UNITY IN FACING THE WORLD

Not only in their relation with one another, but also in their confrontation with the world at large are the churches exploring the possibility of a greater unity. This is well illustrated by the work of the Commission of the Churches on International Affairs. Here is the first attempt to establish an official permanent agency of the churches for dealing with issues of world politics on a more than national basis.[8] The task is one of overwhelming difficulty. Even within a single country, the attitudes, assumptions, and practices of different churches with reference to political matters are diverse enough to be baffling. Indeed, in a single denomination, the views on any concrete issue may represent almost contradictory positions. The differences become vastly multiplied when the effort involves developing a common Christian mind on an inter-

---

[8] A partial—but only partial—exception was the World Alliance for International Friendship through the Churches. During the years between the two world wars it did much to further international contacts among Christian leaders. It was an association of individuals rather than of churches, although a few of its national units had a semiofficial relation to churches.

national, instead of a national, level. This is what was undertaken when the Commission of the Churches on International Affairs was created in 1946.

Statements on international issues in the past, it must be admitted, have often been amateurish in knowledge of political complexities, and therefore too unrealistic to carry much weight. The Commission of the Churches on International Affairs, however, has deliberately set itself to acquiring expert familiarity both with the political arena in general and with particular areas where conflict is threatening. Its personnel includes lay specialists in political science and government as well as theologians versed in the Christian faith and ethic. In its day-by-day operations, its staff maintains strategic contacts in two different directions. On the one hand, it keeps in touch with national church bodies in many parts of the world, both by correspondence and in person, becoming acquainted with their problems and relaying to them the concerns of churches in other lands. On the other hand, it sustains continuing relationships with intergovernmental agencies—like the World Health Organization and UNESCO and particularly the United Nations itself—in order to channel to them such judgments as may arise out of the interchange of viewpoints and experiences among the churches of the world. Not the least important contribution is made through the friendly informal contacts of the Commission with leaders in the United Nations, and the personal assurance that they are supported by the prayers of Christian people in all lands.

The present frustration in world politics, highlighted by the line-up of two great blocs in a "cold war," is so great that it would be visionary to expect the churches greatly to affect the tide of immediate events. What can fairly be said, however, is that the Commission of the Churches on International Affairs has made an auspicious beginning in helping the churches to understand their responsibility in the sphere of international politics, and in a few important matters to register a soundly formulated concern. The best illustrations thus far are in relation to long-range interests of refugees, aid to economically underdeveloped peoples, and problems of population control. In these areas, the churches can speak out of competent knowledge as well as from a sense of moral accountability.

In two ways, the Commission of the Churches on International Affairs marks a definite advance in making Christian influence felt in world politics. First, the fact that it represents the churches not of one nation but of many reduces the danger that what intends to be a Christian judgment will really be only an unconscious reflection of national interests. The nationalistic bias of Christians in one country finds at least a partial corrective when exposed to the nationalistic viewpoints of others, and the prospect of a more objective outlook is thus enhanced. The second point of advance is that by building up a permanent staff of persons who specialize in gaining a cumulative knowledge of political realities, the churches can hope, in due time, to acquire a voice which will command increasing respect. Needless to say, this can be no short-range achievement, but is a matter of years and decades.

PIONEERING IN ECUMENICAL ACTION

In addition to ecumenical aid and ecumenical study, the World Council provides a center for exploring new opportunities of ecumenical action. A welcome instance of this is the work camps for Christian youth each summer. They bring selected young people of different churches of many nations and races together for a month of Bible study and discussion combined with manual labor on a project of constructive service to human need. In 1960, more than one thousand young men and women, chiefly college students, participated in forty-seven camps in thirty-one countries, including such areas of social ferment as Congo, Ghana, Kenya, and Southern Rhodesia. During the years since this program was initiated, more than ten thousand youths have had this kind of enriching ecumenical experience.

Another stimulating project is directed toward a more effective Christian witness by lay men and women. Involved in it is a fundamental rethinking of the meaning of the priesthood of all believers. One of the underlying principles is that the role of the laity is not merely to support the church as an institution, but to *be* the church—the church in its relation to secular society. What the layman does from Monday through Saturday in his occupation or profession, not what he does on Sunday in the church building, is pictured as his primary opportunity of Christian service. The home, the school, the farm, the shop, the factory, the market place, the labor union headquarters, all these are interpreted as places of the church's ministry through its laity. In conventional patterns of thought, the layman assists the clergyman in the work of the church, but in the emerging conception the clergyman assists the layman in extending the work of the church into the world.

These and other efforts for the renewal of the church are undergirded by an original experiment known as the Ecumenical Institute. Made possible by a generous gift of the late John D. Rockefeller, Jr., the Institute is domiciled in a beautiful country house in Bossey, Switzerland, in a rural atmosphere about fifteen miles from Geneva. It is a place of worship and retreat, a conference center and a school of adult Christian education—all combined in one project of training for ecumenical leadership. It brings together Christians of the greatest ecclesiastical and cultural diversities for periods of concentrated attention upon some common Christian interest.

The Institute is conducted on the principle that all who share in the conferences help to educate one another by their interchange of insight and experience. For four months of each year, there is a course of ecumenical study at the graduate level, chiefly for theological students, for which credit may be received from the University of Geneva. During the rest of the year, conferences and consultations, each usually of about a week's duration, are going on. They cover a wide range of Christian concern—missions, evangelism, social work, family life, Christian education, the relation of men and women in the church and society, the healing ministry of the church, Christianity and industry, Christianity and international affairs. Whatever the theme, it is rooted in Bible study and is dealt with from the standpoint of the Church Ecumenical.

From Bossey each year several hundred persons return to their work with a deepened sense of a personal connection with the church as a world community.

By no means least in strategic importance is the function of the World Council in enabling the churches—now in one area, now in another—to deal in an ecumenical perspective with serious crises. Let two concrete cases highlight this unique type of service.

When the Second World War came to an end, there was great doubt as to how soon reconciliation could be brought about between Christians who had been separated by the bitter political struggle. Although at this time the World Council existed in only a provisional form, its staff promptly arranged a meeting with the newly formed Council of the Evangelical Church in Germany. This took place in Stuttgart early in October, 1945. The German group included Bishop Theophil Wurm, Bishop Otto Dibelius, Dr. (later Bishop) Johannes Lilje, and Pastor Martin Niemöller. As one of the participants, I can testify to the poignant nature of the experience. The German leaders drafted a statement, afterward widely publicized, in which they recognized the guilt of the German people for the Nazi regime, and their own share in it. The effect was so reconciling that the moot question of "war guilt," which bedeviled the international relations of the churches for a long time after the First World War, was not a serious problem after the Second.

Another illustration of the strategic role which the World Council plays in conditions of special tension is the current situation in the Union of South Africa. This is an area in which Dutch Reformed and Anglican churches have been almost as isolated from each other for several years as the churches of the Bantu and the white peoples. When in 1960 they became even more sharply divided over some of the issues involved in the government's policy of apartheid, the World Council sent a representative from Geneva to consult with leaders on both sides. As a result, all eight member churches in South Africa, including Dutch Reformed and Anglican and Bantu, agreed to the Council's proposal for an unhurried conference along definite lines. The report of the conferees registered a clear opposition to specific forms of racial discrimination. At subsequent meetings the governing bodies of two of the Dutch Reformed Churches did not sustain the findings of the conference and withdrew from the World Council. But the holding of the conference, under conditions of complete fellowship and frank interchange, serves as a beacon light that continues to shine and illustrates the process by which the World Council brings an ecumenical perspective to bear upon a critical situation involving both ecclesiastical and political aspects.

Unsolved Ecumenical Problems

These concrete pictures of what the World Council is doing may induce too roseate expectations. In the interest of realistic judgment, it is necessary to point out some of the limitations of the present and the uncertainties of the future. In part, these are due to conditions within the ecumenical movement. In part, they arise from factors on the outside.

Viewed from one angle, the tremendous variety of ecclesiastical types within the structure of the World Council is a remarkable triumph of Christian fellowship. Viewed from another angle, it is a formidable hurdle in moving on to a further stage of unity. In this connection, two problems in particular call for such careful examination that the next two chapters (III and IV) will be devoted to them.

One of these problems is the distance between the Protestant and the Eastern Orthodox in their understanding of the nature of the church and of each other. In spite of the steadily growing contacts of friendly appreciation, their doctrine and practice at certain points are so far apart that any real rapport will require much charity and patience. Adding to the complexity of the relationship is the fact that the largest of all the Orthodox bodies, the Church of Russia, is within the Communist orbit and is subjected to totalitarian pressures that may gravely limit its freedom of association.

The other internal problem is the relation of the churches of the West to the churches of Asia and Africa. The crux of the matter is whether the Council—despite its being in name and intention and principle a *world* council—can avoid being overinfluenced by the churches of the West. The great disparity in numerical strength and in financial resources between the churches of the two areas tends to give undue weight to Western viewpoints. Unless this temptation is successfully resisted, what is designed as a world council might turn out to be virtually a Western council with a superficial embroidery of Asian and African color.

In addition to these problems within the World Council, there are even more perplexing issues of relationships with the bodies of Christians that remain on the outside. These are of such weighty import for the long-range future of the ecumenical movement that they will receive extended treatment in subsequent chapters (V and VI).

The first of these enigmatic conditions is the absence of certain large Protestant groups from the ecumenical circle. The Southern Baptist Convention and the Lutheran Church-Missouri Synod come at once to mind. In the case of the Southern Baptists, their decisive emphasis on the complete freedom of the local church and their fear of any kind of centralized authority have led them to decline membership in both the National Council and the World Council. In the case of the Lutherans of the Missouri Synod, their doctrinal conservatism has made them hesitant about becoming associated with Christians of diverse theological views.

Still further removed from ecumenical fellowship are various groups which are often classified under the rather patronizing description of "sects." Many of them may more properly be designated as Pentecostal denominations. They have a common characteristic in their intensive emphasis on the immediate work of the Holy Spirit as the *sine qua non* in the experience of the Christian. Some of them—like the Churches of God, the Assemblies of God, and the Church of the Foursquare Gospel—are of recent origin but have had a rapid growth among people of lesser economic and cultural opportunity, largely unreached by the older, well-established denominations. As long as bodies as important as the Southern Baptists, the Missouri Synod Lutherans, and the Pentecostalists hold aloof, there must be a sadness over the vacant chairs in the ecumenical household.

Furthest removed of all from the ecumenical movement of today is the Roman Catholic Church. Indeed, most Protestants probably think of it as quite unrelated to ecumenical interests. Yet that church is the largest body of Christians in the world. No movement could be fully ecumenical if it ignored Christians of the Roman obedience and felt no pain because of the wide gulf between them and the rest of the Christian world. The fact that Rome has had no ties with the World Council is, of course, due to its own deliberate rejection of them. Today, however, there are many indications of a more sympathetic attitude. Roman Catholic scholars are beginning to publish important and discerning studies of the ecumenical movement. Friendly personal contacts between Roman Catholic and Protestant theologians and biblical students are becoming much more frequent. There is no evidence that the Roman Church will move toward official participation in the ecumenical movement but at least there are gratifying attempts on both sides to understand each other better and to live together as Christian brethren, even though "separated brethren." In the long vista of generations yet to come, this might even prove to be one of the most germinal by-products of the ecumenical movement.

The greatest weakness in the ecumenical movement as we see it today is that it is so largely a concern of national leaders in the denominations, so little an interest of the rank and file of their members. Any accurate balance sheet would show that it has not yet greatly affected the life of the average local church on Main Street. Most congregations are so absorbed in their parochial affairs that their awareness of being vitally related to a world-wide Church is very feeble. In their relation to the churches of other denominations in the same community, there has been an undoubted gain, but this, too, is often a decidedly marginal matter. The indispensable condition of advance for the ecumenical movement as a whole is its domestication within the local church. This is so urgent that we shall consider it at length in a later chapter (VII).

Where Is the Ecumenical Movement Going?

Our review of the last fifty years and our survey of the present scene inevitably raise the question, where is the ecumenical movement going? What is its goal? Can we give any clear answer, or is the movement like the mythical bird which, according to legend, flies backward and so only knows where it has been?

That there is much ambiguity about the long-range destination must be frankly recognized. Two divergent views compete with each other, and each is held by men of ecumenical spirit and devotion. One sees the solution of the problem of unity in terms of increasing *co-operation and fellowship* among the denominations. The other is committed to ultimate *union*.

Neither of these viewpoints looks for a short cut to unity by ignoring the historic rootage of the denominations. That was once the attitude of impatient spirits who thought the scandal of division could be cured by forgetting the past and making a fresh start in an undenominational community church. This approach to the problem of unity has no serious standing in the ecumenical movement. The question is rather whether the denominations, if they continue to work together more and more effectively, are to be accepted as having permanent justification, or whether they should strive for a synthesis of their historic experiences in one visible structure.

On this crucial point, the ecumenical movement has not yet arrived at any general consensus. There is, accordingly, serious confusion as to whither it is headed. Some support it ardently because they see organic union as a possible final goal. Others have misgivings about it for exactly this same reason. Distrustful of big organization and ecclesiastical control, they suspect that union would result in too much centralization and a loss of hard-won freedoms. Still others seek a middle ground where there would be full intercommunion, a ministry and sacraments accepted by all, and an interchangeable membership, but without a union of the denominations in "one great church." For the long road ahead, here is a fundamental question which the ecumenical movement must try to answer, and our final chapter (VIII) will be devoted to it.

Meanwhile, there is common ground on which all who cherish the ecumenical spirit can stand together. All have a "holy dissatisfaction" with the fragmenting sectarianism of the past. All are committed to the quest for some better manifestation of unity than unco-operative and exclusive denominations. All can agree, in the light of fifty years of experience, that whatever goal of ampler unity lies ahead is to be reached on the highway of increasing association in every area of Christian life and thought.

Up to the present time, we have hardly more than touched the outer fringes of what could be achieved by a more whole-hearted co-operation through our councils of churches. Our co-operation is still a peripheral feature of our denominational life, not something that is central and determinative for policy-making and practice. In spite of all the progress that has been made, the denominations still hold back from committing the more important responsibilities to the councils that they have created. Most councils are expected to facilitate useful consultation rather than to exercise the more important functions. The duties that are assigned to councils are often those that involve no denominational advantage. The member churches support a local council, for example, in providing chaplains for prisons and public institutions, or support the National Council in a ministry to migrant workers, or support the World Council in a humanitarian service to refugees. But prisoners and roving workers and refugees are not likely to add much strength to a denomination!

If we really believe that our unity in Christ lies at a deeper level than our differences, we will find more and more ways of manifesting it in common action. As the message of the Lund conference on Faith and Order put it: "Should not our Churches ask themselves . . . whether they should not act together in *all* matters except those in which differences of conviction compel them to act separately?"[9] To move out decisively on such a policy would mean an invigorating change in the ecclesiastical climate. It might then turn out that the co-operation of the last half century had prepared the way for actual union another half century hence.

[9] Tomkins (ed.), *The Third World Conference on Faith and Order* (London: SCM Press, 1953), p. 16.

Chapter III

FELLOW PILGRIMS ON THE ROAD

Asian and African Churches in the Ecumenical Movement

For several years after the initiation of the World Council of Churches, there was reason to wonder whether it would become a truly world-wide Council or would be virtually a Council of the West. In principle, there was never any question about it. In practice, the problem was serious. Would the older and stronger churches of Europe and North America, accustomed to think of Asian and African and Latin American Christians as belonging to "mission fields," make room for them not merely in nominal membership but in a full sharing of responsibility? Would the Younger Churches, still small minorities in their own countries, be prepared to assume active roles in international leadership? Even though both questions were answered in a clear affirmative, could practical problems of administration be handled on a global scale?

Those who were most concerned with the embryonic ecumenical structure desired, of course, that it be world-embracing, and assumed that it would be. But to secure a continuous and effective participation of Christians of all continents meant an organizational task of unprecedented proportions and called for bold strategies. At the lowest level, it involved an increased expenditure of both time and money if leading Christians of Asia and Africa and Latin America were to meet with Europeans and North Americans and Australians often enough to serve as a representative governing body of the Council. At a more important level, there were far-reaching questions as to the present and future relationships of the Younger Churches to the older Christian communities.

The term "Younger Churches" is by no means a satisfactory designation for the Christian communities resulting from the missionary movement. Some of them are actually older than some of the churches of the United States! Moreover, the adjective "younger" may sometimes seem to have an overtone of immaturity. A more accurate description would be "Churches of Asia, Africa, Latin America, and the Pacific Isles." This, however, is so long for constant repetition that we can hardly avoid letting Younger Churches slip into our vocabulary.[1]

PARTICIPATION IN ECUMENICAL CONFERENCES

When the World Missionary Conference was held at Edinburgh in 1910, only seventeen out of more than twelve hundred delegates came from Asia and Africa or from other areas which were then described as mission fields. And not a single one of them came as a representative of a *church*. They were present through appointment by missionary agencies.[2] The Younger Churches were still appendages of the missionary movement.

---

[1] Although this chapter is especially focused on the churches of Asia and Africa, this does not imply that the Evangelical churches of Latin America are of less concern. If we refer to them rather incidentally it is only because they do not have the same kind of colonial background that colors so much of our present discussion. They have a strategic importance of their own as outposts of the ecumenical movement in an area dominantly Roman Catholic. There are six autonomous member churches of the World Council in Latin America, plus Methodist, Anglican, and Disciple bodies represented through their mother churches with headquarters elsewhere. Bishop S. U. Barbieri of the Argentine is one of the presidents of the World Council.

[2] For the full list of those attending in this capacity see W. Richey Hogg, *Ecumenical Foundations* (New York: Harper & Brothers, 1952), pp. 395–396.

In the Continuation Committee created by the Conference to carry out its plans, there were, however, Chinese, Japanese, and Indian Christians—a manifest recognition that there were communities in Asia which were well qualified to be represented not by Western missionaries but by Asian Christians.

When the first conference on Christian Life and Work was held in Stockholm in 1925, its orientation was so completely Western that there were only six representatives of Younger Churches, and none of them was listed as a speaker. At the first conference on Faith and Order, two years later in Lausanne, with an attendance of four hundred, there were only five non-missionary delegates from the Younger Churches—two from India, two from Japan, one from China. As late as the Oxford conference on Life and Work in 1937, only twenty-nine of more than four hundred delegates came from Younger Churches. It was not until the 1938 meeting of the International Missionary Council in Tambaram, South India, that any of the great ecumenical gatherings had a representation from the Younger Churches commensurate with their emerging importance.

At the inaugural Assembly of the World Council of Churches a decade later in Amsterdam, the representatives of the churches of Asia, Africa, and Latin America as delegates, alternates, or consultants numbered fifty-eight, and their participation was substantial. The opening sermon was given by the youthful D. T. Niles of Ceylon. G. Baez Camargo of Mexico and Bishop Y. Y. Tsu of China were members of the business committee. Miss Wu Yi Fang was a member of the committee that drafted the Message. Dr. M. Kozaki of Japan and Bishop C. K. Jacob of India were vice-chairmen of important sections. Miss Sarah Chakko of India chaired the committee on the life and work of women in the church. Professor T. C. Chao of China was one of the six presidents elected by the Assembly. The Younger Churches were much more than an incidental part of the ecumenical family as it came together for its first official Assembly.

The issues faced by the Assembly, however, were primarily

those that were of greatest concern to European and North American Christians. This was due, in part, to the constant presence of the "cold war" between the West and Eastern Europe in the foreground of consciousness; in part, to the fact that the International Missionary Council at Whitby, Canada, a year earlier had dealt at length with major issues confronting the Younger Churches. It was not until the Central Committee of the World Council held its annual meeting in India, in 1952 at Lucknow, that there was conclusive evidence that it was prepared to give as much attention to the problems of the Younger Churches as to the problems of the churches in the West. Since that time, no one could doubt it.

On their side, the Younger Churches have special difficulties in trying to carry a full measure of ecumenical responsibility. In their own countries, they constitute only a tiny minority in a vast non-Christian setting. In Asia as a whole, they are only a little over two per cent of the population—and this figure includes Roman Catholics as well as Protestants. In Japan and Thailand and Pakistan, they are less than one per cent. Even in Korea, they are only a little over five per cent. In most of these areas, the Christian movement has not yet affected the dominant religious cultures very deeply. In such circumstances, the energies of Asian Christians must be directed primarily to strengthening their own position and to bearing a Christian witness in their own immediate environment.

In several countries—like India, Pakistan, and Burma—the churches are confronted by a pronounced renaissance of the non-Christian faiths. The ancient religions have the current advantage of being able to capitalize on the waves of intense nationalism that now sweep across the continent. To be truly an Indian, it is urged, is to be identified with Hinduism as the historic and indigenous faith of India. To be a patriotic Burmese is to support actively the Buddhist heritage. To be a good Pakistani is to be a Moslem. In large measure, this revival of the traditional religions of Asia is a counterattack upon the whole cultural impact of the West.

Reaction against the West

The young Christian churches, just at the time when they have a new opportunity to develop their ecumenical outlook and relationships, must overcome the psychological handicap of being too closely connected with the culture of the West. They have the delicate task of taking their full and rightful place in the Church Universal at the same time when they must leave no room for doubt about their oneness with the nationalistic ambitions of their own peoples. These peoples are throwing off the last vestiges of Western domination. The Christians of these areas must not afford justifiable ground for suspicion that their identification with Christians of the West weakens their rootage in their own national soil.

Westerners cannot understand the almost overwhelming problems of the Younger Churches today without reminding themselves that the great age of Christian missions in Asia and Africa was also the age of a colonialism against which there is now a surging emotional reaction. Asian and African nationalism of today has a pungent anti-Western flavor. Great Christian leaders who are resolute patriots but have had many contacts with the West—such as D. T. Niles of Ceylon or Rajah B. Manikam of India—are likely to be viewed dubiously as westernized Asians. The truth is that in Jesus Christ they have transcended the conflict between East and West, but one can hardly expect this to be understood by the rank and file of their fellow countrymen.

Since the missionary expansion of Christianity into Asia and Africa went on simultaneously with the political and economic expansion of the West into those continents, it is not surprising that the two movements often appeared like related parts of a single development of empire building. The establishment of Christian schools and colleges and hospitals, naturally patterned after the institutions with which the missionaries had been familiar in their own lands, reinforced the impression that missions were an aspect of Western cultural imperialism. To most Africans and Asians today, Christianity still has a foreign "feel," even in places where the church is effectively domesticated. To recognize this should give us a deepened respect and gratitude for the way in which members of the Younger Churches are meeting the double challenge of being ecumenical-minded Christians and devoted patriots at the same time.[3]

In the extreme case of the Chinese Christians under the Communist regime, it has to be admitted that the ecumenical tie is feeble and precarious. Political nationalism seems to find at least a partial parallel in an ecclesiastical nationalism. There are signs, however, that the Christians, having kept the church alive during the cyclonic social revolution, are desirous of re-establishing ecumenical contacts as soon as political conditions will permit. Five of the Chinese churches—the Church of Christ in China, the Anglican, the Baptist, the Congregational, and the Methodist —were related to the World Council when it came into official existence in 1948. Whether they still regard themselves as within the ecumenical fellowship remains to be seen, but Christian leaders from other countries who have had the opportunity of making visits to China bring back reports that allow ground for hope.

New Patterns of Relationships

The present reaction of Asians and Africans against everything Western as a reminder of imperialism—political, economic, social, religious—raises the question whether the end of the missionary era is in sight.[4] If "missionary era" be understood as involving an assumption that a Western Christendom, as the bearer of the Christian ethos, continues to be the "home base" from which its representatives are sent out to peoples of an inferior culture, the answer has to be an unqualified "Yes." No American or

[3] For a penetrating treatment of this situation and its consequences for the world mission of the church, see Lesslie Newbigin, *One Body, One Gospel, One World*.

[4] The statistics do not suggest it. According to a study by the Missionary Research Library in 1960, there are 42,250 Protestant foreign missionaries, of whom 27,219 are from North America.

European missionary has any prestige or influence today in Asia or Africa as an American or a European. On the contrary, his white face and his Western cultural associations are a handicap to him.

But if being missionary means bearing witness to the universality of the gospel, then we may say that the great missionary era has just begun. From this standpoint, every church in every land is involved in the missionary task. Every church in every land is the "home base" of a world-wide mission. Every church—equally in England and in India, equally in America and in Africa—stands in a missionary relationship to the world. It is only a recognition of this missionary situation that can save any church from settling down complacently to ministering to a coterie of congenial people and adapting itself uncritically to its cultural environment. Churches in North America need to be especially reminded that as long as that continent has approximately ten per cent of the world's population and forty-four per cent of the world's income, they can never disclaim a missionary responsibility.

We must never assume that missionaries are important only during the interim period until a Young Church is well-rooted in the native soil. Even when it has reached the stage of being fully able to carry the primary responsibility for evangelizing the people of its area, there is a basic reason why it still needs a Christian witness that can best be given by someone from another land. The reason is that such a witness testifies to the world-embracing and boundary-crossing quality of the Christian faith and the Christian Church as nothing else can do.

The very fact of a missionary's "foreign-ness" is a needed reminder of the universal nature of Christianity and of the church as a reality not tied to any national or racial group. The missionary is in his own person—whatever be the service he renders— a symbol of the truth that the Christian gospel is not an expression of a Western culture or of any human culture, but belongs to a divine order which transcends all the divisive limitations in the life of mankind.

When St. Paul said that he "had been entrusted with the gospel to the uncircumcised, just as Peter had been entrusted with the gospel to the circumcised" (Gal. 2:7) but that the same Lord worked through both, it was precisely this boundary-crossing character of the gospel that he was affirming.[5] There never is a time when, nor a place where, this aspect of Christianity does not need to be stressed. The church is always under the subtle temptation to conform too easily to the standards of the community in which it happens to be set, and even of becoming just a sanction for those standards. The presence of an element in its midst that seems foreign helps to save the Christian community in any nation from yielding to the temptation, and thus makes a vital contribution to its spiritual health. This is as true of the church in America or England as in Japan or Indonesia.

But a new pattern of missionary relationships is called for. In their new circumstances, the Younger Churches can no longer be satisfied to be related to their fellow Christians in other lands through a missionary board or society. This carries too much of the old connotation that they are on the receiving end of a missionary program rather than being responsible partners in it. The churches in India, for example, want to be in direct contact with the churches of the United States and on the same plane with them in the Church Ecumenical.[6] In this situation, the World Council of Churches has a unique place to fill. In its structure, all Christian bodies, young and old, large and small, have the same status. However unequal in resources, they are equal in churchly standing.

From the viewpoint of the churches of Asia and Africa, the newness of the World Council is a further psychological asset. It is so youthful that it does not have a history of identification

[5] I am indebted to Charles W. Forman of Yale Divinity School for the interpretation of this important point about the significance of the missionary movement.

[6] In response to this situation and in order to provide its own constituency with a clearer symbol of the missionary enterprise of today, the former Presbyterian (U.S.A.) Board of Foreign Missions has become the Commission on Ecumenical Mission and Relations of the General Assembly.

with the era of Western colonialism and imperialism. Both of these factors lend strategic significance to the current plan for integrating the International Missionary Council with the World Council of Churches.

ECUMENICAL AND MISSIONARY INTEGRATION

It would not have been surprising if serious tension had developed between the World Council and the International Missionary Council as a result of the relation of each of them, in different fashion, to the Younger Churches. Happily, this has not been the case. From the very beginning of the World Council's life, even in its provisional form, it has had the International Missionary Council as an associated body. Although the two organizations have been officially autonomous, they have worked together in the closest co-operation and have had a joint committee for the furtherance of common concerns. They have shared in the responsibility for several projects, notably the Commission of the Churches on International Affairs and an East Asian secretariat. From the outset of the World Council's life, the prospect of an eventual merger of the two Councils has been in the minds of the leaders of both, and ways and means of effecting it most advantageously have been discussed with increasing favor on both sides.

In these discussions, the weightiest factor has been the recognition of an inherent mutuality of interest. On the one hand, the World Council of Churches, as a movement of Christian unity, has always kept in mind that unity is for the sake of the Christian mission in the world. It has steadily insisted that any movement which was called ecumenical but which was not decisively missionary would be unworthy of the name. On the other hand, the International Missionary Council, as an organ of the missionary enterprise, has constantly stressed the principle that a greater unity is a *sine qua non* for the fulfillment of its objective. These converging viewpoints came to a definite focus at the meeting of the Central Committee of the World Council in Rolle, Switzerland, in 1951, in a statement on "Mission and

Unity." In an oft-quoted sentence, the adjective "ecumenical" was defined as referring to "the whole task of the whole Church to bring the Gospel to the whole world." The concerns of the two Councils were by this time so patently and intimately interlocked that there was little doubt that in due season they would become one body.

On both sides, however, the procedures were cautious for practical reasons. Among the missionary groups, there were those who feared that a complete union of the two bodies might result in a less emphatic challenge to the specific task of missionary extension. This was especially true among some of the European missionary societies, which were not closely connected with churches and which doubted whether the churches in their corporate life were missionary-minded enough to sustain a robust missionary program. In the World Council's circle, on the other hand, the Eastern Orthodox churches had misgivings about including missionary responsibilities in its program. This was chiefly due to the assumption that Protestant missions involved proselytism in the homelands of Orthodoxy.

After long and patient study, the complete integration of the two Councils now seems assured. Under the plan formulated by the joint committee and approved for submission to the Assembly of the World Council in New Delhi, India, November 18–December 5, 1961, the International Missionary Council ceases to have a separate existence and becomes the World Council's Division on World Mission and Evangelism.

The organizational problem involved in this integration of the two bodies has been a difficult one because of their different types of structure. The International Missionary Council is based upon the national (or regional) Christian councils in lands of the Younger Churches and upon the national conferences of missionary agencies in the lands of the older churches. In the World Council, on the other hand, the only member units are the churches themselves in the lands of both East and West. Under the plan of integration, the World Council remains strictly a council of *churches*, the members of its Assembly being composed exclusively of official representatives of the churches. Within the Division of World Mission and Evangelism, the national Christian Councils and national conferences of missionary agencies continue to have the supervisory responsibility that they formerly had in the International Missionary Council.

The significance of this organizational union lies at a deeper level than the co-ordination of functions. It is found in the principle that the church in its essential nature is both ecumenical and missionary. It is ecumenical because of its origin in one universal Lord. It is missionary because that Lord has entrusted to it the universal proclamation of the gospel. Its unity is for the sake of its mission to the world. And its mission to the world includes witnessing to the unity of the Christian community in relation to the one Lord. Since church and mission thus belong together, the World Council of Churches and the International Missionary Council belong together.

Each of the Younger Churches, as a result of the historical circumstances of its origin, has usually been intimately related only to the missionary agency of a single denomination of a single country. This one-track line of contact has inevitably had a restrictive influence. Under the new pattern which the union of the World Council and the International Missionary Council effects, the Younger Church will more naturally think of itself not as on the receiving end of a denominational or national program but as a responsible partner in the mission of the world-wide church as a whole.

It may be that the World Council, after its integration with the International Missionary Council, will have a key role in the missionary program. It is clear that the Christian world mission would be in a far stronger position in Asia and Africa if it had an ecumenical base instead of national and denominational bases. These will continue to be essential for educational promotion and financial support, but as the channel of communication between older churches and younger they are woefully outdated. It is contrary to both the spirit and the constitutional structure of the World Council to claim any administrative function for itself, but it might turn out that the member churches would one day deliberately ask the World Council to undertake a major missionary responsibility in their behalf.

Regional Responsibility

In the process of finding their place in the ecumenical movement, the Younger Churches have been coming into a closer relation with one another. Until recently, the churches of Asia were almost as separated from one another as from the churches of the West. Today, a hopeful form of regionalism is emerging which is in large measure a by-product of the ecumenical development.

An early contribution to the regional development was the appointment of Rajah B. Manikam in 1949 to be the representative both of the World Council and of the International Missionary Council in East Asia. He became a roving ambassador among the many small churches of the area, building up a closer fellowship among their leaders and between them as a group and the ecumenical movement.

These informal, personal contacts took on a more established form when an East Asian Christian Conference was held in Prapat, Indonesia, in March, 1957, to consider the common tasks of the churches of that great area. This conference signaled the arrival of a new stage of regional responsibility. It was the first assembly of churches of lands outside Western Christendom that was planned and directed entirely by themselves. It explored especially their evangelistic opportunity and duty in East Asia. The missionary movement was now appearing not as something that moved from a base in the West into Asia but as something for which the churches of Asia were also responsible and which had its base wherever there was a community of Christian people.

A pregnant fact not yet realized by most Western Christians is that several Asian churches are already achieving a missionary outreach beyond their own borders. The United Church of the Philippines has twelve missionaries in other parts of Asia. The

Methodist Church in the Philippines has four. The Korean Presbyterian Church has two. Indonesian and Japanese churches also have the beginnings of a foreign missionary program. The Mar Thoma Orthodox Church in India has several scores of Christian workers outside its own territorial and language limits of Malabar. It is increasingly anomalous to describe such churches as "younger." They have come of age.

What was initiated at Prapat was established on a permanent basis in May, 1959, at Kuala Lumpur, Malaya, when a constitution for the East Asia Christian Conference was officially adopted. Thirty-four denominations and fourteen national Christian Councils were represented. A continuing secretariat was created, with D. T. Niles of Ceylon as general secretary, Kyaw Than of Burma as administrative secretary, and Alan Brash of New Zealand as secretary for interchurch aid. The organization is autonomous, wholly responsible to the churches of the region, but in intimate association with the ecumenical movement as a whole. At the Kuala Lumpur meeting, W. A. Visser 't Hooft, speaking in behalf of the World Council of Churches, urged the East Asians to speak up vigorously if they should ever feel that it was acting like a Western council. Spokesmen of the East Asian churches, on the other hand, strongly emphasized their intention not to be a geographical bloc but to maintain constant co-operation with the World Council.

It does not take much prophetic vision to realize that what is happening in this new development may prove to be of the highest strategic importance for world-wide Christianity. Asia has more than half the population of the world. The era of Western dominance in that continent is over. The future of Christianity in Asia is going to be determined by the leadership which Asian Christians give. Beyond this, it may even prove true that the future of the Christian movement in other parts of the world will be deeply affected by what the churches of Asia are and do.

This budding of regionalism in an ecumenical setting is not limited to the East Asian scene. It is appearing also in Africa, where the new spirit of independence is likely to provide a rich soil. An

All-Africa Christian Conference, the first of its kind, met in Iba-
dan, Nigeria, in January, 1958, with representation from all the
African countries except the Spanish colonies. It is too early to
forecast the long-range consequences, but it is encouraging that
a provisional committee was appointed to carry on after the conference, with a Zulu educator as its executive and with headquarters in Northern Rhodesia. Among the special problems to which
it is addressing itself are the relation of the African churches to
the revolutionary economic and political changes, the uprooting
of tribal peoples by modern technological developments, the splin-
tering of Christianity into many isolated sects, and evangelization
in the face of a Moslem advance.

Another region in which the Younger Churches are beginning
to move closer together in order to deal with common problems
is Latin America. Ecumenical developments here have been excep-
tionally slow, owing partly to the fact that a large percentage of
the Protestants are of Pentecostal types, individualistic in temper
and unaccustomed to meeting and praying together. Plans are
gradually getting under way for an All-Latin-American Conference.

The regional principle and the ecumenical principle might be
conceived theoretically as in conflict with each other, but in practice they supplement and strengthen each other. A regional conference provides the method by which the churches of a given
area can make their fullest contribution as a group to the ecumenical movement and receive the most help from it. By reason of a
common historical background and a common cultural setting,
they have problems which do not press with equal insistence upon
Christians of other areas, even though the world-wide Christian
community has a real stake in them.

The churches of East Asia, for instance, confronted by religions
of a pantheistic type, face the dangers of religious syncretism more
sharply than other churches do. The churches of the Middle East
have a distinctive orientation because of their common encounter
with Islam. The Evangelical churches of Latin America face special problems of their own as minorities in a region where Roman

Catholicism has long been dominant. The churches of Europe face common issues arising from the tradition of established linkage with the state. The churches of North America have their common difficulties for precisely the opposite reason—the strong historical emphasis on the separation of church and state and consequently an extreme religious pluralism. In each case, the churches of the area need to wrestle together with their own characteristic problems, but to do so in a clear awareness that what they decide is of concern to the Christian movement as a whole and also that they may learn from the experience of other parts of the Church Ecumenical.

The first Assembly of the World Council of Churches was held in Europe, the second in North America. The third is being held in Asia. The pattern is thus set for subsequent assemblies in Africa, in South America, in the Antipodes, in the Pacific Isles. Such gatherings are visible symbols not only of the world-wide character of the Christian community but also of the significance of regional interests and of the role which the Younger Churches are increasingly playing in the ecumenical movement.

YOUNGER CHURCHES AND CHURCH UNION

The rise of the Younger Churches has been one of the most potent influences in the direction of a greater unity in the Christian movement as a whole. Most of the missionaries were not interested in extending their denominational borders. Their concern was to proclaim the gospel to the world and to demonstrate its universal quality. Their work resulted, however, in transplanting the ecclesiastical divisions of the West to the rest of the world. In the lands where these divisions had their origins, they might still have contemporary significance, but in the wholly different settings of India or Japan or Nigeria the divisions were not only an irrelevancy but an obscuring of the difference between Chris-tian and non-Christian faith. The issues confronting the new churches in the midst of Hinduism and Buddhism and Islam were of a very different order from the historical differences of the Western churches. For the Younger Churches of Asia or Africa to be separated from one another by factors that had nothing to do with their witness as Christians in a non-Christian milieu was too great a handicap to be borne without protest.

As a consequence, some of the most urgent voices in behalf of union have come from the Younger Churches. These voices were heard as early as the Edinburgh missionary conference of 1910 and rose to a crescendo at the Madras (Tambaram) conference of 1938. At the Lausanne conference on Faith and Order in 1927, Bishop V. S. Azariah of Dornakal in South India bluntly said in a moving interpretation of the attitude of the Younger Churches:

Force of habit, financial dependence, denominational training and, above all, loyalty to their spiritual fathers, now keep them in denominational connections. But these circumstances can not keep them apart forever. . . . The divisions of Christendom may be a source of weakness in Christian countries, but in non-Christian lands they are a sin and a scandal.[7]

The description of denominational divisions in India as "a sin and a scandal" may sound too harsh in our Western ears, but hardly so in a country in which the Christian Church was trying to bear a potent witness against the divisiveness of the age-old caste system.

At the sessions of the International Missionary Council in Madras in 1938, after the conference as a whole had drafted a statement recommending co-operation, delegates of the Younger Churches made a declaration of their own which went far beyond the official utterance. Emphasizing their "passionate longing" not only for greater co-operation but also for "visible union," they appealed to the missionary societies and the authorities of the older churches

to take this matter seriously to heart, to labor with the Churches in the mission field to achieve this union, to support and encourage us in all

[7] H. N. Bate (ed.), *Faith and Order: Proceedings of the World Conference, Lausanne August 3-21, 1927* (London: SCM Press), pp. 493, 495.

our efforts to put an end to the scandalous effects of our divisions and to lead us in the path of union.[8]

Who could honestly say that this earnest plea has yet been taken "seriously to heart"? Many missionaries have given devoted leadership to various projects of church union, but the general attitude of the Western churches has been one of indifference or hesitation. As recently as 1956, a distinguished leader of the Church of North India, Augustine Ralla Ram, felt impelled to declare, after reflecting on an extended visit in the United States:

The Church in that land seemed to say to me, "We will be as ecumenical as you like as long as you do not touch our denominational homes and as long as you leave us alone in these dugouts of ours."[9]

It is neither accidental nor incidental that the most comprehensive union of churches yet achieved anywhere in the world has taken place not in the West, in spite of its resources in leadership and experience, but in South India. In 1919, a small group of ministers of different denominations met in Tranquebar to consider methods of evangelism. This led to what is known as "the Tranquebar Manifesto" in which they said:

We face together the titanic task of the winning of India for Christ —one fifth of the human race. Yet, confronted by such an overwhelming responsibility, we find ourselves rendered weak and relatively impotent by our unhappy divisions—divisions for which we were not responsible and which have been, as it were, imposed upon us from without, divisions . . . which we do not desire to perpetuate.[10]

Twenty-eight years later, after patient negotiations, the united Church of South India came into official existence.

The Church of South India embraces traditions as diverse as the Anglican, the Methodist, the Presbyterian, the Reformed, and the

[8] *The World Mission of the Church: Findings and Recommendations of the International Missionary Council, Tambaram, Madras, India* (New York: International Missionary Council, 1939), pp. 130–131.

[9] *Ecumenical Review*, April 1956, p. 244.

[10] Bengt Sundkler, *The Church of South India* (London: Lutterworth Press, 1954), p. 101.

Congregational. It has, for the first time, bridged the wide gulf that separates churches that insist on the historic episcopacy and those that once rejected it. If Anglican, Methodist, Presbyterian, Reformed, and Congregational churches can thus unite in South India in order to bear a clearer witness to one Lord, what are the implications of this for the future of Anglican, Methodist, Presbyterian, Reformed, and Congregational churches in America and Great Britain?

At the present time, decisions are being made upon even more far-reaching proposals for union in North India, in Pakistan, and in Ceylon. In these negotiations, Baptists and Disciples are involved in addition to the groups included in the Church of South India. If these plans should be consummated, two historic separations would be bridged by Younger Churches at the same time—those occasioned by differences over both baptism and the ministry.

Since the question of episcopacy looms large in most discussions of any comprehensive union, it is instructive to note the different solutions of the problem in the South India and in the North India plans. In South India, the ministers of all the churches came into the united Church on a basis of equality, with an agreement that thereafter all ordinations would include a laying on of hands of bishops and ministers. There was a provision for assuring to each congregation for thirty years the kind of ministry to which it had hitherto been accustomed, with the understanding that at the end of this interim period for growing together, the Church as a whole would decide whether episcopal ordination would be the future pattern for all ministers. In North India, Pakistan, and Ceylon, on the other hand, there is no arrangement for an interim period, but all ministers are brought into a common ministry at the outset through a ceremony commissioning them all for their future service in a united Church. This ceremony, which provides for a mutual laying on of hands, is described as being not a re-ordination but an extension of ministerial service.

In other areas of the Younger Churches—notably Japan, China, and the Philippines—unions have also been effected, though on a scale less inclusive than in South India. Unhappily, it has also to be recorded that in some countries, particularly in South Africa and more recently in Korea, fissiparous tendencies are strong, owing partly to theological and partly to personal factors. Moreover, many of the Asian and African churches are linked more tightly to their mother churches in the West than to their sister churches in their own area. Japanese Anglicans, for example, are closer to British and American Anglicanism than to the Kyodan, the church which unites Christians of several major groups in Japan. This is a situation with which churches of the West need to have a soul-searching concern, since they have been chiefly responsible for it.

If the movement toward union continues to gain strength among the Younger Churches, the future policies of the world-wide confessional organizations may become an acute issue. Are they prepared to see their tie with the Younger Churches become less close in order that the unity of the Younger Churches with one another in their homelands may become stronger? Is the Lutheran World Federation, for example, ready to say, "We are not only willing but eager that in South India the Lutheran churches should become a part of the united Church even though this means that their relation to the Lutheran World Federation becomes wholly secondary"? Is the Lambeth Conference ready to proceed on the assumption that Anglicans in Japan have more in common with Presbyterian and Methodist Christians in that country than with Anglicans as Anglicans in England or in the United States? These are momentous questions. Their answer cannot be postponed without weakening ecumenical Christianity. Upon their answer hangs much of the future strength of the Younger Churches. For them, the decisive issues are not between different Christian denominations but between Christianity and the reviving non-Christian religions.

In structural terms, the question is whether the ecumenical Christian community of the future is to be a world-wide fellowship of strong national churches or whether the world-wide confessional bodies will keep so firm a hold on their denominational units that united churches in national areas will never come into existence. To arrive at the right answer to the question requires each denominational organization to give prayerful heed to our Lord's word: ". . . unless a grain of wheat falls into the earth and dies, it remains alone; but if it dies, it bears much fruit" (John 12:24).

Chapter IV

MORE FELLOW PILGRIMS
ON THE ROAD

Eastern Orthodox in the Ecumenical Movement

One of the richest harvests of the ecumenical movement is the growing fellowship between Protestants and the Eastern Orthodox. Until recently, they were living in widely separated worlds. They had almost no firsthand knowledge of each other's life. On both sides, the image of the other was so stereotyped and distorted that there was not even an interest in knowing more or in having closer contacts.

Probably my own point of view has been fairly typical of the Protestant attitude. There was little in either my education or my earlier experience to lead me to appreciate the church that has had the longest continuous development of any of the Christian bodies. My textbooks in church history made little or no reference to Eastern Orthodoxy after the Great Schism between East and West in 1054—or at least after the fall of Constantinople in 1453. I assumed that the Orthodox Church was static and impervious to renewal, weighted down under the dead hand of the past. I thought of it as preoccupied with an endless repetition of ancient rituals unrelated to the ongoing currents of life in today's world.

The practice of invoking the saints and reverencing icons appeared to me to be expressions of unenlightened credulity. The ascetic and monastic forms of life looked like outmoded medievalism. The long centuries of subservience of church to the state struck me as intolerable. A sacramental mysticism seemed to me to have taken the place of a prophetic mission in contemporary society.

Not until I began to share in ecumenical gatherings and to have personal friends among Orthodox priests and theologians and lay-men did I discover among them a dimension of Christian faith and devotion that I had wholly failed to recognize. Through these later relationships, I have gradually come to be grateful for spirit-ual treasures that are especially characteristic of the Orthodox Church. Among these are deeper understandings of worship as sheer adoration, of the communion of the saints as a vital reality, of the values of a cherished ancient tradition, of the potency of a mystical piety.

An Ecumenical Overture

A good introduction to the role of the Orthodox in the ecu-menical movement is a bit of modern history of which most Prot-estants are unaware. It is that the first official proposal for a permanent association of the churches of present-day Christendom came from Eastern Orthodoxy. In January, 1920, an encyclical letter from the Ecumenical Patriarchate in Constantinople was addressed "unto all the Churches of Christ wheresoever they be," inviting them to consider the formation of a "fellowship (Koi-nonia) of Churches." The drafting of the letter was primarily the work of Archbishop Germanos, who twenty-eight years later was to become one of the first co-presidents of the World Council of Churches. The Patriarchate being vacant in 1920, the letter was signed by the Locum Tenens and eleven metropolitans. One sen-tence in it was so unconsciously anticipatory of what was to come in the World Council that the language is worth close attention:

Our Church is of the opinion that a closer intercourse with each other and a mutual understanding between the several Christian Churches is not prevented by the doctrinal differences existing between

them, and that such an understanding is highly desirable and necessary
and in many ways useful in the well-conceived interest of each one of
the Churches, taken apart and as a whole Christian body, as also for
preparing and facilitating the complete and blessed union which may
some day be attained with God's help.[1]

From the standpoint of the influences that led to the actual formation of the World Council of Churches, this overture was not
of major significance. More dramatic factors, such as the Edinburgh missionary conference, the Stockholm conference on Life
and Work, and the Lausanne conference on Faith and Order,
affected the course of events much more directly. But the letter
was remarkable, even epoch-making, as evidence that the thou-
sand-year-old isolation between Eastern and Western Christianity
was breaking down.

Implicit in the letter was the suggestion that Eastern Orthodoxy
could in practice have a greater flexibility than its dogmatic position logically called for. The Orthodox Church conceives itself
to be the one true Church of Christ, embodying in itself the
wholeness of the Christian faith. Yet this communication of the
Patriarchate addressed other Christian bodies as "Churches of
Christ wheresoever they be" and intimated a willingness to meet
them on a plane of mutual responsibility.

The letter proved to be a forerunner of active participation by
Eastern Orthodox leaders in the planning for both the Life and
Work and the Faith and Order conferences. When the preparatory meetings for the two projects were held in Geneva in the
summer of 1920, Orthodoxy was well represented. This was especially true of the Faith and Order meeting, to which there came
no fewer than eighteen Orthodox from the Greek and Balkan
churches, the Russian Church in Exile, and the Patriarchates of
Constantinople and Alexandria. This wide representation was due
in large measure to a personal visitation of the Orthodox churches
by a delegation from the Episcopal Church of the United States
a year earlier. As a result of the consultations in Geneva at this

[1] The text is given in full in G. K. A. Bell, *Documents of Christian Unity,
First Series, 1920–1924* (London: Oxford University Press, 1924), pp. 44–48.

early stage, an official connection of the Eastern Orthodox with
both Faith and Order and Life and Work became an assured
reality.

At both the Stockholm conference on Life and Work in 1925
and the Lausanne conference on Faith and Order in 1927, there
were impressive delegations from the Orthodox world. At Lausanne, however, they felt it necessary to abstain from voting on
any of the reports with the single exception of the one on "The
Church's Message to the World." In explaining their position to
the conference they affirmed plainly that "the mind of the Orthodox is that reunion can take place only on the basis of the common
faith and confessions of the ancient undivided Church of the seven
Ecumenical Councils and the first eight centuries." "The most
which we can now do," they added, "is to enter into cooperation
with other Churches in the social and moral sphere on a basis of
Christian love."[2]

Again, at the Oxford conference on Life and Work in 1937 and
at the Edinburgh conference on Faith and Order in the same year,
the Orthodox were well and ably represented. At Edinburgh,
there were twenty-seven Orthodox from thirteen churches and
also ten representatives of the "Lesser Eastern Churches"—Armenian, Coptic, Abyssinian, Syrian. Once more, the Orthodox group
found it necessary, although not refraining from voting, to register their doctrinal divergences along the general line of their
earlier statement at Lausanne.

THE ORTHODOX IN THE WORLD COUNCIL

When the World Council of Churches finally came into existence at Amsterdam in 1948, several of the Orthodox bodies were

[2] This, it is interesting to note, reflected a different point of view from
that voiced by the Moscow consultation of Orthodox representatives held
in 1948, who criticized the ecumenical movement for dealing too much
with issues outside the dogmatic and spiritual realm. For a more detailed
account of the relation of the Eastern churches to the ecumenical movement
in the twentieth century see Ruth Rouse and Stephen C. Neill (eds.), *A
History of the Ecumenical Movement* (Philadelphia: Westminster Press,
1954), chap. 14.

officially represented, including the Greek-speaking churches, the Russian Exarchate in Western Europe, and the Orthodox groups in the United States. None of the Orthodox within the Communist orbit participated, and probably some of the other Orthodox churches had been deterred by the unfavorable judgment passed on the ecumenical movement by the Orthodox consultation in Moscow a few weeks earlier. Viewing Orthodoxy as a whole, one would have to say that its share in the Amsterdam Assembly was very limited. It was now clear, however, that vigorous groups within Orthodoxy were determined to maintain an active cooperation in the World Council, indicated by Archbishop Germanos' acceptance of the role of one of the co-presidents.

The presence of the Eastern Orthodox in the World Council has a significance that can hardly be exaggerated. Without them, its fellowship would be virtually pan-Protestant rather than ecumenical. Except for the relatively small Old Catholic group,[3] the Eastern churches constitute the one Christian family in the Council that has no historic tie with the Reformation. Their membership is the most convincing evidence that the Council cherishes both the Catholic and the Protestant traditions and does not confine its outlook and its concern to Protestantism.

From the standpoint of practical strategy and statesmanship as well as of Christian comprehensiveness, the relation of the Orthodox to the ecumenical movement is of extraordinary moment. In a large part of the world, including both the area where Christianity was cradled and nearly all of Eastern Europe, the future of the Christian Church as a whole stands or falls, humanly speaking, with the Orthodox. This is, of course, notably true of Russia. Although there are groups of Protestants in Russia, particularly Baptist and Lutheran, no one can doubt that if the Christian Church is to make any strong impact in that great domain it will be through the renewal and strengthening of the Russian Orthodox Church.

[3] The Old Catholic Church was formed by a withdrawal from the Roman Catholic Church as a protest against the decrees of the Vatican Council of 1870, especially the promulgation of the dogma of the infallibility of the Pope.

THE ORTHODOX IN RUSSIA

Although our understanding of the situation in Russia is too limited to permit any forecast of future developments, we can at least say that the church has kept its faith alive during the greatest ordeal that any church of modern times has had to undergo. If we are inclined to criticize the Russian Church for its limitations, we may well recall the story of the man who was asked what he had done during the French Revolution. His laconic reply was, "I survived." The single fact of the survival of the Church of Russia during the more than forty years since the revolution should temper the judgment of those who condemn it for restricting its activity to the maintenance of public worship and conforming to the policies of a totalitarian state controlled by an atheistic party. No group of Christians in the world, unless it be the young church in China, has a stronger claim than the Church of Russia upon the prayers of Christians everywhere.

The attitude of the Church of Russia toward the ecumenical movement is still extremely cautious, but the first steps have been taken toward what may prove to be a responsible relation. At least, the mood is markedly different from the cold aloofness shown when the World Council was established in 1948. At that time, the consultation of representatives of Orthodox churches held in Moscow in connection with the five hundredth anniversary of the autocephalous existence of the Church of Russia[4] took a wholly negative position—a position in conspicuous contrast with the earlier attitude of Orthodox leaders outside the Russian orbit of influence. The conference, under the obvious guidance of the Russian Patriarch, alleged that the ecumenical movement "no longer attempts to secure the reunion of the Churches by spiritual ways and means," but directs its efforts "into the channels of social and political life."[5]

[4] The description of the Orthodox Churches as "autocephalous" is their way of indicating that although they hold a common faith and order, there is no centralized government. The several national groups are administratively autonomous.

[5] Quoted by Nicolas Zernov, *A History of the Ecumenical Movement,* p. 667.

In the light of this judgment, the Church of Russia did not become a member of the World Council. The leaders of the Council, however, never took the decision as final. Ten years later, a limited degree of contact was established, as the result of informal conversations in Utrecht in August, 1958, between representatives of the Moscow Patriarch and of the World Council. A few months later, there was an extended visit of two Russian Orthodox leaders to the headquarters of the World Council in Geneva. In the summer of 1959, Russian Orthodox observers (without vote) attended for the first time the meeting of the Council's Central Committee on the Island of Rhodes. This tentative "feeler" was followed later in the same year by a visit of a five-member delegation from the World Council to the Patriarchate in Moscow in the interest of further mutual understanding. Again, in 1960, Russian Orthodox observers met with the Central Committee of the Council in St. Andrews, Scotland. This led in 1961 to an official application for membership, which will be considered by the New Delhi Assembly.

In none of these preliminary contacts have the representatives of the World Council tried to make things smoother by avoiding the points of greatest difficulty. They have felt under an impulsion not only to seek for a path of Christian reconciliation but also to bear a true witness to ecumenical principles, including the responsibility of the churches in the social and cultural sphere.

Outside the Communist orbit, significant ties were being forged at a much earlier date with the smaller and freer Orthodox groups in America. As far back as 1924, the Federal Council of the Churches of Christ in America had established a "Committee on Relations with the Eastern Churches," based largely on the friendly contacts that had developed through the work of Near East Relief in the period during and after the First World War. In 1938, one of the smaller Orthodox groups in America, the Syrian Antiochian, joined the Federal Council, the first Orthodox body to become a full-fledged member. Its example was followed by the Ukrainian Orthodox Church of America in 1943 and the Russian Orthodox Catholic Church of North America in 1944.

Since then, the Greek, the Romanian, the Serbian Orthodox in the U.S.A. and the Syrian Orthodox in America have established official relations with the National Council of Churches. The fact that all these have become members of the National Council is a gratifying demonstration that it is possible to preserve distinctive traditions while entering into a growing fellowship and co-operation.

POINTS OF TENSION

That there are real tensions between Protestant and Orthodox, even within ecumenical circles, goes without saying. To most Protestants, the Orthodox priest—even more the monk—is still a remote and unfamiliar figure. The Orthodox liturgy, conducted in an unknown tongue, seems to them almost devoid of spiritual value, and the veneration of the Virgin Mary and the saints seems definitely unevangelical. For the Orthodox, on the other hand, there are even graver difficulties in their ecumenical relations. To them, the bustling busyness of Protestants and the Protestant unconcern with the tradition of the early centuries are signs of a superficial understanding of the Christian faith and of the Christian Church. Moreover, when the Orthodox representative joins his Protestant brethren in ecumenical gatherings, he feels under practical handicaps. He finds himself in a minority group in the midst of a majority whose characteristic ethos is different. The discussions are carried on in languages—English, French, German— in which he probably is not at home, and that makes it hard for him to present his own contribution or to be sure that he understands the contribution of others.

A practical point of much psychological strain has been the "proselytism" carried on by some of the Protestant bodies in lands which the Orthodox have regarded as their area of special responsibility. The Orthodox see it as a serious breach of Christian fellowship when anyone who has been baptized in the Orthodox Church is persuaded to join a Protestant body. The Protestant churches in the Balkans and the Middle East have been chiefly formed, in an earlier era, out of converts who had an Orthodox background, and the critical attitude of the Orthodox toward this fact is understandable. The member churches of the World Council, however, today disavow any proselytizing purpose in relation to the Orthodox. As a result of a clarifying study of "Christian Witness, Proselytism and Religious Liberty," carried on by the World Council's Central Committee over a period of several years, it seems probable that this issue will occasion much less strain in the future.

Largely as a result of the resistance of the Orthodox to proselytism as they have understood it, there has been a prejudice in Orthodoxy against anything which bore the label of "missions." It has come to sharp focus in the discussions of the integration of the International Missionary Council and the World Council of Churches. This prospect the Orthodox viewed with misgiving. They saw it as tending to give missionary societies too much influence in World Council affairs. This tension, however, is likely to be of only temporary duration, for of course the Orthodox are not opposed to missionary activity in the sense of carrying the gospel to all non-Christian people. As a matter of historical fact, the Greek Orthodox Church has a magnificent missionary record of having won the Slavs to the Christian faith. During their long period of political subjection to the Turks, the Greek and other Christian communities in the Balkans were not permitted to carry on missions in our sense of the term, but they were always aware of a duty of Christian witness through life and worship, and clung to their Christian tradition with great tenacity.

The basic source of theological tension between Orthodox and Protestant lies in their divergent conceptions of the church. How can those who believe the Orthodox Church to embody in itself the fullness of faith and already to possess the true unity intended by Christ reconcile this conviction with the kind of recognition of other churches which is involved in joining with them in a Council of Churches? The logic of the Orthodox position was expressed by the Orthodox delegates to the North American Conference on Faith and Order at Oberlin in September, 1957, when they insisted on recording the view that "all Christian groups outside the Orthodox Church can recover their unity only by entering into the bosom of that Church which preserved its identity with early Christianity."[6]

On the face of it, this position looks as dogmatically rigid as that of Roman Catholicism. Yet in practice there is a radical difference between the two. In spite of a theoretical exclusiveness, the Ecumenical Patriarchate could, as we have already seen, officially propose a "fellowship of Churches," and many of the Orthodox bodies have subsequently followed the course to which the proposal pointed by joining the World Council. As is so often the case in human affairs, when an abstract principle is confronted by concrete realities at variance with it, the interpretation and application of the principle are gradually modified. Although not surrendering their conviction about the nature of their church, the Orthodox are certainly dealing with other churches as parts—even if imperfect parts—of the Body of Christ.

An event that has greatly helped to foster a better understanding on both sides was the decision of the Ecumenical Patriarch in 1955 to seek a more direct tie with the World Council of Churches by appointing a representative to serve as his liaison at its Geneva headquarters. In the person of Bishop James of Melita, who four years later (as Archbishop Iakovos) was to be appointed the head of the Greek Archdiocese of North and South America, this relationship became very important. His participation in the day-by-day discussions and planning in Geneva became so mutually helpful that what began as an experiment has become a permanent arrangement between the Patriarchate and the Council.

A public evidence of the strengthened bond was the statement made by the Ecumenical Patriarch in the midst of the confused situation when Pope John XXIII announced in Rome, early in 1959, that he would convene an Ecumenical Council which would consider problems of Christian unity. In view of the intimation that reunion with the Orthodox might be one of its special concerns,

[6] For the full text of the statement see Paul S. Minear (ed.), *The Nature of the Unity We Seek: Official Report of the North American Conference on Faith and Order* (St. Louis: Bethany Press, 1958), pp. 159–163.

the Patriarch made a clear declaration that the Orthodox would be willing to be represented at such a Council "only if the entire Christian world is invited to send representatives." He also added that in such an event "the minimum representation" of non-Roman Churches should be "their collective representation through the World Council of Churches."[7]

An important milestone on the road of better understanding between Orthodox and Protestant leaders was the holding of the 1959 meeting of the World Council's Central Committee on the Island of Rhodes. This was the first time a session of the official governing body had been held in an area of strong Orthodox tradition and influence.

LEARNING FROM EACH OTHER

On the Protestant side, several things have been learned as a result of the increasing *rapprochement* with the Orthodox. For one thing, it has become clear that a church with a hierarchical order does not necessarily have a highly centralized government. In fact, Eastern Orthodoxy is very much like Protestantism in always facing the difficult problem of getting sufficient administrative authority to enable it to function as a whole in any responsibility. The Eucumenical Patriarch, as a bishop who is *primus inter pares*, is recognized as the highest spiritual leader of Orthodoxy, but he has no canonical jurisdiction over the national or regional branches of the church. Each of them has full administrative powers in its own area. The bond of unity among them is not external but is a common tradition which they all cherish, including a common conception of church order and a common liturgy. The principle of organization among the national churches is federative, not monolithic, and there is no continuing organ for the definition of doctrine or the detailed guidance and discipline of the faithful—nothing corresponding to the papacy of the Roman Church or to the Vatican.

---

[7] As quoted by Archbishop Iakovos in an article entitled "The Contribution of Eastern Orthodoxy to the Ecumenical Movement," *Ecumenical Review*, Vol. XI, No. 4 (Geneva, July, 1959), p. 403.

There is, accordingly, within Eastern Orthodoxy a possible adaptability and diversity in procedural matters which is closer to a Protestant than a Roman Catholic type of structure. The lack of any legal external authority leaves a more diffused area of freedom for the present-day leading of the Holy Spirit.

The highest organ of authority in Eastern Orthodoxy is the church itself—the consensus of the whole community of the faithful in its collective life. Such a consensus is registered not by bishops or priests but only through an Ecumenical Council of the entire church.[8] In this respect, again, there is, in principle, a measure of parallelism with Protestant views. For twelve centuries, however, there has been no Council of Eastern Orthodoxy as a whole, and because of crippling political conditions under which most of the Orthodox have had to live—and still have to live—the holding of a Council representative of Orthodoxy in its entirety has been beset and still is beset with insuperable difficulty.

Another point at which many Protestants have gained a better understanding of Orthodoxy has to do with the nature of tradition. Protestantism has made a sharp contrast between Scripture and tradition, insisting that Scripture alone is authoritative. To call anything "traditional" even invests it with an unfavorable connotation in the Protestant mind! The Orthodox, on the other hand, glories in tradition. To him it implies the church of the Apostolic Age, the church of the saints and of the great Fathers in the faith, the Ecumenical Councils in the centuries of an undivided church. The Holy Tradition, as interpreted by the Orthodox, is based on the Bible but is held to be equally authoritative with the Bible. For the Orthodox, Holy Bible and Holy Tradition go together: there is no conflict between them.

There is undoubtedly an issue of critical importance here. Those who are heirs of the Reformation will always find in the Bible the decisive norm of spiritual authority. This is because it is the only record of God's self-communication in Jesus Christ. The Bible is thus the anchor that keeps the church from drifting away from its

---

[8] Some Orthodox scholars, however, interpret the Orthodox position as attributing special authority in matters of doctrine to the hierarchy.

permanent base in Christ. But the disparagement of tradition by Protestants has often been superficial and extreme. As a matter of fact, there are no churches whatever that do not depend on tradition. It is one of the inevitable facts of historical life. Our creeds and our forms of worship are all matters of tradition. As a distinguished Lutheran scholar observes, "The very principle of *sola Scriptura* is itself a tradition."[9] And a stanchly biblical Presbyterian like James Moffatt could even entitle one of his books *The Thrill of Tradition,* and speak of "the throb of being in contact with some living truth or force which is older and larger than ourselves, embodied . . . in symbols, rites and usages."[10]

In the case of any particular practice or belief, the issue is not whether it is tradition, but whether it is a tradition that is consistent with the revelation in Christ as we know Him through the Bible. In the living stream of the church's life, under the guidance of the Holy Spirit, Scripture and tradition cannot be dissociated, since there is always the question how Scripture is to be understood. A tradition created by spontaneous generation or by an arbitrary fiat must indeed be rejected. But this is very different from rejecting the whole principle of tradition. If we see validity in the principle, we may then go on to consider with our Orthodox brethren whether any particular point in the Holy Tradition is at variance with what has been given us in the Christ of the Scriptures.

A New Dimension in Worship

It is probably in the realm of worship that Protestants are learning most from their contacts with the Orthodox. The genius of the Orthodox Church is that it is a worshiping community standing in adoration before the glory of God. Included in this worshiping community—the communion of the saints—are not merely those who are visible in the flesh but all the faithful of all the ages. In the experience of worship, the Orthodox feel time to

[9] Jaroslav Pelikan, "Where's the Log for Dialogue?" *Pulpit Digest,* November, 1959.
[10] New York: The Macmillan Company, 1944, p. 3.

be transcended and the human condition to be transfigured by the divine. Earth and heaven, time and eternity, meet. For the Orthodox, it is not a figure of speech but an experienced reality that "with all the company of heaven we laud and magnify Thy glorious name."

Of this quality of Orthodox worship, the Protestant who is present for the first time at a rendering of the liturgy may be quite unaware, although even then he can hardly fail to be thrilled by the heavenly music. As he becomes more familiar with the Orthodox worship, he discovers a mystical sensitivity which enlarges his own earthbound vision. He begins to understand the conception of "ecumenicity in time," to use a phrase of the Russian Orthodox scholar, Professor Georges Florovsky. To all Christians, being ecumenical involves an awareness of a Christian fellowship that embraces men and women of all nations and all denominations, but to the Orthodox it has the additional meaning of a fellowship that embraces all the Christian faithful of all the generations.

Something of this distinctive atmosphere of Orthodox worship is indicated by the decisive importance of the Resurrection for the Orthodox. It has a central place in both experience and theology hardly matched in either Protestantism or Roman Catholicism. It is more than accidental that some of our greatest Easter hymns have an Orthodox origin. To one of the great Fathers of the Eastern Church, John of Damascus, for example, we owe both

> The Day of Resurrection,
> Earth, tell it out abroad . . .

and

> Come, ye faithful, raise the strain
> Of triumphant gladness! . . .

For the Orthodox, these are not merely "Easter hymns," but expressions of the very heart of Christian faith and life.

To most Protestants, the Orthodox type of experience seems very "otherworldly." The Orthodox do not object to its being thus characterized. It *is* otherworldly. Less, however, in terms of a future world in contrast with the present than of a heavenly world that invades the earthly scene and glorifies it. As an Orthodox theologian puts it, in speaking of the sacraments, the icons, and the saints, "the splendor of eternity breaks into the reality of today."[11] An infusion of this kind of otherworldliness into the extreme this-worldliness of most of American Protestantism would contribute a new dimension of experience.

The Protestant criticizes the Orthodox for a too passive attitude toward the evils of the present world. Many of the Orthodox today accept the criticism as having a large measure of validity. It is certainly true that through the centuries the Orthodox Church has not been marked by the prophetic social vision that challenges the existing state of affairs and releases energies for changing it. This is to be understood, at least in part, in the light of the environing circumstances under which Orthodoxy has had to live. During a great span of its life, it has been under the domination of political power that left little or no opportunity for exerting a direct influence on society.

In the period of the Byzantine Empire, the Eastern Church might, indeed, have exercised a greater freedom from political control. During the long era when they were under Moslem domination, however, a strong Christian witness in the social order was wholly impossible. During the Czarist domination in Russia, something of the same condition prevailed even though the Czars were nominally Christian. Instead of blaming Orthodoxy for its failure in socio-ethical judgment, we should be grateful that at least it kept a light of Christian faith burning in the darkness. The oppressive situation reinforced the tendency to otherworldliness, but it was an otherworldliness without which Christianity might have succumbed entirely. In some respects, it was an otherworldliness like that of the early Christians who were a feeble minority in the Roman Empire yet knew themselves to be a colony of heaven.

It would be a great mistake to imply that Protestantism and Eastern Orthodoxy are, after all, not very far apart. In basic character, the Eastern Orthodox is a church of sacramental mysticism.

[11] Stefan Zankov, *The Eastern Orthodox Church* (Milwaukee: Morehouse Company, 1929), p. 103.

It puts its emphasis on transcending the given state of things rather than upon changing it. It is, to use Paul Tillich's phrases, more concerned for "the consecration of reality" than for "the transformation of reality." Yet Protestant and Orthodox, as they meet in the ecumenical movement, are learning from each other. The Protestant discovers in the Orthodox a deeper understanding of the contemplative aspects of Christian piety. The Orthodox finds in the Protestant a stronger sense of Christian social responsibility. This mutual give-and-take within the Christian fellowship is fraught with creative possibilities for the church as a whole.

Chapter V

ROADS THAT DIVERGE

Non-co-operating Protestants and the Ecumenical Movement

Although the last fifty years have seen a remarkable strengthening of the forces making for unity, several important groups of American Protestants give little evidence of being affected by it. Conspicuously absent from the list of co-operating denominations, as pointed out earlier, are the Southern Baptist Convention and the Lutheran Church-Missouri Synod. Other smaller bodies, especially concerned with doctrinal orthodoxy of the kind which they describe as "evangelical," are negative or critical in varying degrees in their attitude toward the ecumenical movement.

Still other groups, often ungraciously called "sects," have come into being within this same period and have been too absorbed in their own development to give thought to their relation with the older Protestantism. The distinctive preoccupation of many of them with the role of the Holy Spirit tends to make them a class by themselves, often described as Pentecostal.

These vacant chairs in the ecumenical household are so significant as to call for sober reflection. It is important to understand why such earnest companies of Christian people are on the outside.

Southern Baptists

The Southern Baptists are a great and growing denomination, numbering more than nine millions of members in more than thirty-one thousand congregations.[1] In the whole of American Protestantism, they are the second largest group. In considerable areas of the South, they are as numerous as all the other bodies of Christians taken together. In recent years, under an aggressive missionary program, they have moved out from the Southern states into other parts of the nation—the midwest, the north, and the Pacific Coast. They have not hesitated to establish competitive churches even in communities where there were already strong congregations affiliated with the American Baptist Convention.[2] In spite of resulting tensions, the Southern Baptists have continued to maintain this policy. Their success in "going it alone" has confirmed them in the practice.

For any understanding of Southern Baptist aloofness from the ecumenical movement, the first requisite is an appreciation of the importance which all Baptists attach to the independence of the local church. This position the Southern Baptists hold in an extreme form. A revealing illustration of it occurred at the Oxford conference on Church, Community, and State in 1937. A distinguished Southern Baptist scholar, Dr. James R. Sampey, who was in personal accord with the trend of most of the discussions, felt it necessary to explain why Southern Baptists would find it especially difficult to accept the proposal for a World Council of Churches. For the Southern Baptists, he said, there was no such entity as a "church" in the meaning implied in the term "World Council of Churches." There was, of course, "the Church" in the general spiritual sense of the whole family of believers but the only "church" of an organized and functional character was the gathered group of Christians in the locality where they lived and

[1] *Yearbook of American Churches for 1960* (New York: National Council of Churches, 1959), p. 253.
[2] The organization of Southern Baptists as a separate convention goes back to 1845 when they withdrew from what was then called the General Missionary Convention of Baptists, chiefly over the question of slavery.

worshiped. In strict Baptist principle, therefore, as he went on to expound, the Southern Baptist Convention is not a church, and there would be no way by which Southern Baptists could join a world-wide Council of Churches except by the vote of thousands of autonomous congregations.

The same point of view was expressed more officially by the Southern Baptist Convention a few years later in declining the invitation to join the World Council. "Our Convention," it was stated, "has no ecclesiastical authority; it is in no sense the Southern Baptist Church."[3] The logic of the argument was weakened by the fact that the Convention was already a member of the Baptist World Alliance through a decision made by the Convention, not by the congregations. The incident, however, indicates how strong is the Southern Baptist feeling about local autonomy.

The insistence on the complete independence of the congregation has made Southern Baptists ultra-cautious about anything that looks like a centralized authority or administration. The necessities of effective action, however, have led them to develop strong administrative agencies for their denominational work in missions and education and other activities. In practice, the relation of these agencies to the local church differs little from that which prevails in other Protestant bodies. But the Southern Baptist conviction of the great dangers of overhead direction makes them highly susceptible to the fear that such a drawing together of ecclesiastical bodies as the World Council of Churches or the National Council of Churches represents might lead to a loss of freedom.

In fact, a Council of Churches rests on the very principle of voluntary fellowship which Southern Baptists magnify. The constitution of the World Council explicitly forbids it to legislate for the churches. To "offer counsel and provide opportunities of united action in matters of common interest" is the limit of its constitutional function. Emphasizing this point, the Central Committee of the Council at its meeting in Toronto in 1950 unequivocally disclaimed any other role than that of servant of the

---

[3] No fewer than eleven Baptist bodies in different parts of the world have subsequently become members of the World Council of Churches.

churches. There is still, however, a lingering misgiving among Southern Baptists that the ecumenical movement in all of its expressions is in some vague way a threat to liberty. It is not uncommon even to hear the intimation voiced that the World Council might become some sort of a "Protestant Vatican." By a happy lack of consistency, however, the Southern Baptist Sunday School Board has long been helpfully related to the Uniform Lesson Committee, which is a unit in the National Council's Division of Christian Education.

In spite of the general lack of contacts on a denominational basis, many Southern Baptists share in co-operative projects and conferences. In their own communities, Southern Baptist congregations are increasingly joining in local councils of churches. In Indonesia, to take an illustration from a different kind of situation, the Southern Baptist mission has contributed to the interchurch aid program of the Indonesian Council of Churches. Hosts of Southern Baptists are ecumenical in spirit and would not oppose participation in either the National Council of the Churches of Christ in the U.S.A. or the World Council of Churches if it were clear to them that this did not imply any relaxing of their Baptist testimony or of their freedom of action.

One of their esteemed leaders, Professor Theron D. Price, of the Southern Baptist Theological Seminary in Louisville, summarized well the current attitude of many of his thoughtful colleagues in a symposium in preparation for the Oberlin study conference of 1957 on "The Nature of the Unity We Seek." After emphasizing the principle that each local church is independent, he continued:

At the same time the churches are interdependent; and this requires to be expressed in association and cooperation. . . . It is the writer's feeling that we Southern Baptists are in much greater danger, at present, of failing to make our witness to the Whole Church by isolation than of losing the distinctiveness of that witness by association. . . . But it would be difficult to convince us that the visible reduction of the mystical body [of Christ] to one legal corporation would enhance the true unity of the Church. In whatever measure this is even a subsidiary aim of the leadership of the World Council of Churches, it will be met with a stubborn resistance by Southern Baptists.[4]

MISSOURI LUTHERANS

In the case of the Lutheran Church-Missouri Synod, its lack of ecumenical relationships has been chiefly due to an entirely different factor—its rigidity in doctrine. Missouri Synod Lutherans are not unconcerned with the unity of the church, but they have insisted that there must be agreement in the statement of doctrine as a prerequisite of either co-operation or union. Efforts to secure even the limited measure of unity that goes with any project of co-operative fellowship are often characterized as "unionism," and unionism has been a pejorative term among them.

It is not surprising that Missouri Synod Lutherans have held aloof from the ecumenical movement, for their special emphasis on doctrinal purity has kept them from being full members of even the National Lutheran Council and the Lutheran World Federation. If it is so difficult to co-operate with fellow Lutherans it is, of course, more difficult to find common ground with non-Lutheran Christians. There are evidences, however, of a growing disposition to take a place within the ecumenical circle.

At the Oberlin conference on "The Nature of the Unity We Seek" in 1957, the Lutheran Church-Missouri Synod was represented by observers, the first time it had shared in ecumenical discussions of Faith and Order. In 1958, the publishing house of the denomination gave a dinner in recognition of what had been done by the staff of the National Council of Churches in providing a testimony of public worship in the national parks. In 1959, there were two unprecedented official decisions: first, to assume membership in the Division of Home Missions in the National Council of Churches; second, to send observers to the next Assembly of the World Council of Churches.

In an important article written as a part of the study process that preceded the Oberlin conference, a distinguished professor at

[4] "A Southern Baptist Views Church Unity," *Christian Unity in North America*, J. Robert Nelson (ed.) (St. Louis: Bethany Press, 1958), pp. 86–88.

the Concordia Theological Seminary of the Lutheran Church-Missouri Synod, Dr. Richard R. Caemmerer, gave an interpretation of "unity in doctrine" which affords hope that the impasse between that church and the ecumenical movement may be overcome. Citing the frequently quoted clause of the Augsburg Confession which declares that "for the true unity of the Church it is enough to agree concerning the doctrine of the Gospel and the administration of the sacraments," he suggests that this does not mean that there must be "identical propositions" *about* gospel and sacraments. Instead, he sees the Confession as insisting that there must be agreement "with one accord to think and work *for* the teaching of the Gospel and the administering of the sacraments."[5] The Confession is thus construed as holding that unity arises when Christians concentrate on the communication of the Word to the world. Dr. Caemmerer's article may be a signpost pointing to new possibilities of understanding between the most conservative of the Lutherans and the ecumenical movement.

THE EVANGELICALS

Outside the ecumenical movement as thus far developed, there are Christian groups that co-operate with one another but not under the aegis of the World Council or the National Council of Churches. They lay claim to the special designation of "Evangelicals." In America, they are organized for common action in the National Association of Evangelicals, formed in 1942. On the international level, they participate in a loosely knit consultative body known as the World Evangelical Fellowship, established in 1951 with headquarters in London. Neither the national nor the international body is strictly a council of denominations, since both include various organizations as members but each provides a rallying point for Christians who in varying degrees are out of sympathy with the ecumenical movement.[6] In America, the Na-

[5] "Church Unity and Communication," *Christian Unity in North America*, pp. 98–102. Italics mine, S. McC. C.

[6] To complete the picture, a brief reference should be made to the so-called American Council of Christian Churches, organized in 1941. Numerically unimportant, it is an association of the most combative

tional Association of Evangelicals has been generally critical. In Great Britain, the Evangelical Alliance is more tempered in its attitude; in 1958, it made a statement which "readily acknowledges the value of certain functions" of the World Council of Churches.

The Evangelicals place their primary emphasis on maintaining doctrinal orthodoxy as they understand it. They regard the basis of the World Council of Churches, which affirms faith in Jesus Christ "as God and Saviour," as an insufficient theological foundation for co-operation. The requirement for membership in the National Association of Evangelicals covers agreement on a series of specified points, including the Bible as the infallible word of God, the Trinity, the virgin birth of Christ, His personal return to earth, regeneration by the Holy Spirit as a necessity, the present ministry of the Holy Spirit, the resurrection of both the saved and the lost, and the spiritual unity of believers.[7]

To set "evangelical" over against "ecumenical," as leaders of the Evangelicals insist on doing, is highly confusing on both sides. On the one hand, many of those in the "Evangelical" camp are truly

---

Fundamentalists gathered around the controversial figure of Rev. Carl McIntire. After being dismissed from the ministry of the Presbyterian Church in the U.S.A. in 1936 on charges of disturbing the peace and unity of the church, he became the head of a small dissident group known as the Bible Presbyterian Church, which later split apart over the issue of his leadership. In 1948, he took the initiative in creating an International Council of Christian Churches, whose main stock-in-trade has been implacable opposition to the World Council of Churches and the International Missionary Council. His reckless and wholesale allegations of "apostasy," "modernism," and "Communism" within the churches of the ecumenical movement are not taken seriously outside his own little circle of extremists. As conservative a publication as *Christianity Today* summarizes the matter pithily in the comment of its executive editor, on April 28, 1958, that "the cause of Christ has suffered greatly at the hands of those who, proclaiming their orthodoxy to the skies, have shown themselves totally lacking in Christian love, courtesy and forbearance." For more detailed information see Ralph L. Roy, *Apostles of Discord* (Boston: Beacon Press, 1953), chaps. 8, 9, 10.

[7] For a detailed presentation of the doctrinal position of N.A.E. see J. Marcellus Kik, *Ecumenism and the Evangelical* (Philadelphia: Presbyterian and Reformed Publishing Society, 1957).

ecumenical. On the other hand, hosts of Christians in denominations
that are members of the World Council of Churches regard themselves as firmly evangelical in the fullest sense of the word. Moreover, several churches of the World Council have always had the
adjective "evangelical" explicitly and proudly in their names. This
is true, for example, of the Evangelical United Brethren, the Evangelical Church in Germany (Lutheran), the Evangelical Synod of
Syria and Lebanon, and the Union of Protestant Evangelical
Churches of Belgium. No group can monopolize so great and historic a word as "evangelical." Since, however, a particular organization currently applies the term to itself, we can hardly avoid
using it in their fashion in our present discussion.

Typical of the criticism of the ecumenical movement by Evangelicals is J. Marcellus Kik's *Ecumenism and the Evangelical*.[8] As
the most thorough attempt to give a systematic analysis of the
Evangelicals' attitude, it calls for special attention. Kik registers
five main grounds of misgiving. They are: (1) The fear of centralization and something like a "super-Church"; (2) the failure to
recognize explicitly the authority and inerrancy of Scripture; (3)
the lack of a creedal statement and the "minimizing of theology";
(4) the "inclusiveness" of the World Council and the National
Council, leaving the way open for "liberals" to become leaders in
them; (5) too great a concern with the visible organization of the
church as against a "spiritual unity."

Ecumenical enthusiasts may regard such criticisms as negligible,
but it is salutary to examine them seriously. They are certainly the
convictions of many sincere Christians who are not to be written
off as either obscurantists or obstructionists.

For the present separation between the "evangelical" and the
"ecumenical" Christian, the responsibility is not all on one side.
Nor is the gulf between them as unbridgeable as some on both
sides assume. Each has something to learn from the other. The
necessary condition of a *rapprochement* is a better mutual understanding of the real situation. The first stage in this understanding
is frequent and frank conversations with each other as Christian

[8] *Op. cit.*

brethren instead of a stubborn entrenchment in two separate camps.

In such a give-and-take of insight and experience, it might become evident that the misgivings entertained by Evangelicals rest on possible dangers of which the ecumenical movement needs to be alertly aware. At the same time, it would surely be discovered that the misgivings are vastly exaggerated and do not reflect what is actually taking place in ecumenical circles. A brief comment on each of Kik's five criticisms may help to make this clear.

CRITICISM BY EVANGELICALS

1. The Evangelical fear of overcentralization undoubtedly has historical support. There is plenty in the record of the church through the centuries to warn us to be constantly on guard against a concentration of administrative control and a curtailment of creative freedom by institutional authority. But those who know the ecumenical movement from the inside would unhesitatingly say that this is a danger which has been in the forefront of its thinking from the beginning. It is evident not only in the provision of the World Council's constitution which forbids it to legislate for the churches and in the amplification of this by the Toronto Declaration of 1950, but also in the entire development of its policies over the subsequent years. Indeed, the very genius of the Council lies in its effort to achieve a form of unity which can be dynamic and effective without centralized controls.

2. The criticism of the ecumenical movement for not explicitly affirming the authority of Scripture has a measure of justification. If there were such an avowal in the World Council's constitution, it would be a stronger document for its purpose. But the lack of such a formula in the constitution by no means involves a lack of biblical foundations in the Council. Any examination of either its documents for study or of the reports of its Assemblies will provide overwhelming evidence that the Scriptures actually are taken as the authoritative standard. In fact, nothing has been more noteworthy in the development of the Council than the influence of Bible study and biblical theology on its thought.

This does not mean that all participants in the Council's program describe the authority of the Bible in the same way. They would not all say, for example, that the Scriptures are inerrant in factual data. They are surely at one, however, in holding (in the language of the Westminster Confession) that "the whole counsel of God concerning all things necessary for His own glory, man's salvation, faith and life, is either expressly set down in Scripture or by good and necessary consequence may be deduced from Scripture."[9] There has been much discussion within the World Council concerning an amendment to the constitution which would give formal recognition to what is in actual practice its authoritative use of the Bible, and this is included in the revision of the basis of membership being considered at the next Assembly.

3. The criticism of the ecumenical movement for minimizing the significance of theology overlooks the fact that although there is no list of specified doctrines as a basis of membership, there is an active theological concern throughout its whole life. Doubtless the criticism has arisen because both the Life and Work movement and the International Missionary Council tended in their early days to bypass theological issues as too divisive and to concentrate on co-operation and fellowship in service. From 1936 onward, however, as Life and Work and Faith and Order began to come together to form the World Council of Churches, the theological interest within the ecumenical movement as a whole has been pronounced. Indeed, it would be a fair appraisal of the last quarter century to say that some of the most vital and robust theological discussion in Christendom has found its focus in studies and reports of the World Council.

This theological concern, it is true, does not manifest itself in a formal creedal statement in the World Council's Constitution. This is in keeping with the clear conviction that the ecclesiastical definition of doctrine and the maintenance of doctrinal integrity are the function of the member churches themselves. For a Council to attempt pronouncements of creedal orthodoxy for the

[9] Westminster Confession of Faith, I:6.

churches would be moving precisely in the direction of a super-church—something which Evangelical critics fear! The World Council has accordingly confined its constitutional basis to the single signpost that has served as the rallying center of historical Christianity, namely, the acknowledgment of Jesus Christ "as God and Saviour."[10] This phrase may be open to question on two grounds: first, that it inadequately expresses the richness of the Trinitarian tradition; second, that although it explicitly affirms the deity of Christ, it is not equally explicit as to His true humanity. An amplification of the constitutional basis has been the subject of study since the 1954 Assembly. As drafted by the Central Committee for consideration by the next Assembly, Article I reads as follows:

The World Council of Churches is a fellowship of Churches which confess the Lord Jesus Christ as God and Saviour according to the Scriptures and therefore seek to fulfil together their common calling to the glory of the one God, Father, Son and Holy Spirit.

4. Whether the "inclusiveness" for which Evangelicals criticize the ecumenical movement is blameworthy or praiseworthy depends on what content is put into the term. If "inclusiveness" implies an amiable tolerance toward any and all opinions or an assumption that all are equally valid, it is, indeed, to be avoided. If, on the other hand, it means a serious effort to grasp the *wholeness* of the Christian faith and experience, "inclusiveness" is surely a badge of honor. It is in the latter sense that the ecumenical movement is inclusive. It recognizes that every development within the history of the church has been but a partial comprehension of the richness of truth and life as manifested in Christ. It is therefore eager to discover what the different types of Christian thought and experience have to contribute to the total understanding of

[10] In the National Council of the Churches of Christ in the U.S.A., the phrase is "Divine Lord and Saviour." The two wordings are generally regarded as equivalent. The phrase used by the National Council was taken over from the constitution of the Federal Council as drafted in 1905. The phrase employed by the World Council was the one that appeared in 1910 in the first proposal for a World Conference on Faith and Order.

His gospel.[11] St. Paul's warning against setting up party cries (I Cor. 3:3–11) has constantly to be borne in mind, whether the parties bear denominational names or such other labels as "liberal" or "fundamentalist" or "evangelical." The great dividing line is not between Christians who interpret Christ in different ways but between men who believe and men who do not believe that in Him God has entered into human history for our redemption.

5. The Evangelical's distrust of "organizational" unity as contrasted with "spiritual" unity raises the crucial issue of the nature of the church. All must agree that unity of the spirit in mutual love and trust is the reality that alone gives significance to any unity of institutional structure. But it does not follow that the latter is unimportant. On the contrary, the more we become aware of a unity of the spirit, the more we must be concerned that it be expressed in a way which makes Christians themselves conscious of it and which the unbelieving world can recognize. To profess a spiritual fellowship, for example, while unable to meet together in the deepest act of communion in the Lord's Supper suggests how unrealistic it is to make a sharp separation between unity of the spirit and its manifestation in visible forms and practices.

The Evangelical's criticism often seems to assume that the primary interest of the World Council of Churches is the external unification of the Protestant denominations—or of all Christian bodies—into one vast organization. This is a wholly erroneous assumption. Although numerous individuals may think of church unity in this superficial way, the fundamental ecumenical concern is very different. That concern is the oneness of the People of God, which is His gift to us in Jesus Christ and which Christians are accordingly required to manifest to the world in some convincing way. To discover what that way is, is the *raison d'etre* of the ecumenical movement. As this becomes more widely understood, we may hope that the gap between the "evangelical" and the "ecumenical" Christian will be bridged.

[11] For a further development of this line of thought, see the excellent little book by Oliver Tomkins (now Bishop of Bristol), *The Wholeness of the Church* (London: SCM Press, 1949).

THE PENTECOSTALS

Partly within, but more largely outside, the organized Evangelicals there is a considerable sector of relatively new Protestant
bodies commonly called Pentecostal. Most of them have emerged
during the last half century—the same period in which the older
denominations have been growing together in the ecumenical
movement. The Pentecostal groups have thus far had only slight
contact with mainstream Protestantism and are inclined to be very
critical of the prevailing institutional forms of religious life.

Full of evangelistic and missionary zeal, several of these Pentecostal groups have had a phenomenal growth. They have been especially successful in winning adherents from the strata of society
most neglected by the older churches—those of the lowest levels
of income and of least educational and cultural opportunity.

The term "sect" is commonly applied to bodies of this type. As
used sociologically, the word has no invidious connotation, although many Christians in the more firmly established denominations take lofty attitudes toward such late arrivals on the religious
scene as the Assemblies of God, the Churches of God, and the
Church of the Foursquare Gospel. Viewed in historical perspective, the "sect," in one of Ernst Troeltsch's classic descriptions, is
"composed of strict and definite Christian believers bound to each
other by the fact that all have experienced 'the new birth.' "[12] As
distinguished from the older "churches," the "sects" that we are
considering in our present discussion have certain characteristic
tendencies. These include: (1) a narrowly exclusive viewpoint toward other types of Christians; (2) an emotional heightening of
religious experience; (3) an interest in moral perfectionism or
"holiness"; (4) a rejection of various "worldly" practices; (5) a
primary emphasis on the direct and present activity of the Holy
Spirit.

While there are no over-all statistics that can be cited, a fair
estimate of the groups that are generally regarded as Pentecostal,

[12] *The Social Teaching of the Christian Churches* (New York: The
Macmillan Company, 1933), p. 993.

or at least resemble them in important respects, would probably give the surprising figure of close to five million in North America. In Latin America, they are a major influence in Protestantism. In Chile, for example, the Pentecostal Church has about four hundred thousand adherents and is the strongest Protestant body in the continent.

As a concrete illustration of the Pentecostal sector of Protestantism, consider the Assemblies of God. Growing out of a series of revivals in the early part of this century, they were officially organized in 1914. After an existence of hardly fifty years, they now claim a membership of more than five hundred thousand.[13] There are congregations in every state of the United States and in sixty-nine different countries. For the last five years, the Assemblies of God record an average of two hundred ninety new congregations annually.

The most distinctive aspect of the Assemblies of God is an insistence on "the gift of tongues" as an evidence of the baptism of the individual by the Holy Spirit. A minister who doubted the reality of this experience could not be in good standing. Other characteristics of the group are the practice of healing through prayer and an emphasis on holiness in the sense of separation from "worldly" amusements. The theological viewpoint is that of a biblical literalism.

Although the Assemblies of God magnify the immediate activity of the Holy Spirit as their cardinal principle of faith, they have developed institutional structures similar to those found in the older churches, including national agencies for home missions, foreign missions, Sunday School work, evangelism, and radio work. There is a Pentecostal World Conference which meets triennially, drawing the Assemblies of God into fellowship with groups of a similar viewpoint. The total number of Christians loosely related to this world-wide Pentecostal gathering may be as large as eight million.[14]

[13] *Yearbook of American Churches for 1960*, p. 15.
[14] David J. du Plessis, "Golden Jubilee of Twentieth Century Pentecostal Movement," *International Review of Missions*, April 1958, pp. 193–206.

The Seventh-day Adventists illustrate an older group in interesting contrast with the Pentecostals. The Adventists go back to
the eighteen-forties and owe their origin to an expected imminent
and visible return of Christ to earth. Their study of the Scriptures
also led them to observe the seventh day of the week as the Christian Sabbath. Their foreign missionary ardor is unsurpassed. Their
per capita giving for missionary work, although Adventists are far
from being in the higher brackets of income, is the highest of any
body of American Christians. They number over a million in the
world as a whole. In Colombia today, they are the largest body
of Protestants.

Among the more extreme groups, there may be bizarre figures
—shouting revivalists, sensational faith healers, and jazzy singers of
sentimental gospel songs. Many Pentecostal congregations are still
in the stage of meeting in storefronts or houses. As they secure a
firmer rootage in their communities, they become less sharply
marked off from other Christians, will feel more at home with
them, and may begin to join in co-operative undertakings.

Although the groups which we are considering differ widely
among themselves, there is one special feature which they have
sufficiently in common to justify classifying them together. This
is the crucial importance which they attach to the Holy Spirit as
an active reality in their life today. This accent is so central that
it marks them as a distinctive theological and ecclesiastical type.

We need to be reminded, however, that from the beginning, the
Reformation had its more thoroughgoing and "sectarian" wing,
represented by the Anabaptists and the Mennonites, who went far
beyond the "classical" Reformers—Lutherans, Calvinists, Anglicans—in the emphasis on direct guidance by the Holy Spirit.[15]

[15] If we were reviewing the whole history of the church, it would be
important to point out that the difference between "church" and "sect"
goes back to the very early days of Christianity. The Montanists of the
second century were a noteworthy example of the latter type, stressing
the spiritual value of charismatic gifts and spontaneous response as against
the more stabilized life of the larger Christian community. The same tendency has subsequently appeared over and over again. The issue between
"ardor and order," to use John A. Mackay's arresting phrase, is constantly
recurring in Christian history.

With this went a view of the church as essentially an intimate fellowship in the Spirit, and this involved a sharper break with the old ecclesiastical order. This aspect of the Reformation has seldom received the attention it deserves. It is too little realized, for example, how strong its influence has been in the development of Protestantism in America. Not only Baptists, Mennonites, Quakers, Brethren and Moravians, but in varying degrees and ways Methodists, Churches of Christ and Disciples owe a large part of their genius and outlook to the Anabaptist tradition. In the United States, the Protestants who belong to denominations that stem from this more radical wing of the Reformation, or at least have been greatly affected by it, outnumber Lutherans, Presbyterians, and Anglicans by considerably more than two to one. At least half of the Protestant leadership in the world-wide missionary movement, from the days of William Carey on, has also come from the heirs of the more radical Reformers.

THE ROLE OF THE HOLY SPIRIT

What has happened to the recognition of the Holy Spirit during the course of the Christian centuries has been vividly epitomized by Henry P. Van Dusen in what he calls "on the whole, a pathetic and tragic story." Some of his broad generalizations may need to be qualified a bit, and we must not forget the aberrations to which a one-sided preoccupation with a subjective apprehending of the Spirit has led. His historical summary, however, of the attitude of the church toward the doctrine in successive periods calls for serious reflection:

The indubitable centrality of the Holy Spirit in the life and message of the Earliest Church.

Its regnancy in the faith and thought of the Apostle Paul.

Its capture and imprisonment by Catholic ecclesiasticism.

Its release and renewal in every epoch of spiritual revival.

Its re-imprisonment by the classic Reformers within the text of Scripture.

Its emancipation with power by the so-called "Radical Reformation," the "Reformation sects."

Its gradual quiescence into innocuous conventionality in their later respectability.

Today, its reappearance in familiar excess and wonted power in the contemporary "sects."[16]

This revival of primary emphasis on the Holy Spirit is currently stimulating considerable rethinking in ecumenical circles about the nature of the church. An impressive example of this is found in Bishop Lesslie Newbigin's *The Household of Faith*.[17] Instead of accepting the traditional twofold classification of the Catholic and the Protestant conceptions of the church as an adequate analysis, he insists that there is a third which must always be kept in view. The Catholic magnifies the visible institution as carrying on the mission of Christ. The Protestant of the classical tradition magnifies the message of the church—its understanding of the Word of God and the gospel. The third type, the Protestant of the Pentecostal viewpoint, magnifies the experience of the Holy Spirit as the thing which is really constitutive of the church. It is this latter type of Protestant which is least identified with the ecumenical movement.

The difference among the three types is etched in sharper outline by asking, Where is the church? The Catholic—Greek, Roman, or Anglican—would reply, "The church is where there is historical continuity with Christ through the succession of His accredited representatives." The Protestant of the classical type would reply, "The church is where the gospel is truly proclaimed and the sacraments rightly administered." The Protestant of the more Pentecostal type would reply, "The church is where the Holy Spirit is present."

Of course, neither the Catholic nor the classical Protestant would question the importance of the Holy Spirit in the church. But they do not keep it in the forefront of their thinking. Neither of them has been accustomed to regard the presence and power of the Holy

[16] *Spirit, Son and Father* (New York: Charles Scribner's Sons, 1958), pp. 125–126.
[17] New York: Friendship Press, 1954, especially chap. 4, to which I am greatly indebted in the present discussion.

Spirit as the determinative and decisive thing, the factor that really constitutes the church as church. It is at this point that the Pentecostal bears his most clear-cut witness. He is a reminder that for the church to be the church involves a reality of another dimension than either good order or good doctrine.

If the ecumenical movement is to represent the *wholeness* of the church, it will take fuller account of this type of churchmanship than it has thus far done. There is no reason for undervaluing either the Catholic concern for historic continuity or the Protestant concern for the gospel. There is reason, however, to give more attention to the Pentecostal testimony to the direct activity of the Holy Spirit today. The Catholic's right order of the church and the Protestant's right proclamation of the Word will both be sterile without a constant sensitivity to the empowering Spirit.

The role of the Pentecostals is forcefully set forth in an unforgettable illustration used by Bishop Newbigin.[18] When a prospector, he comments, first strikes oil, there is a tremendous upburst of the new fuel. It burns fiercely until it is brought under control. It is then pumped in a steady flow through pipes and refineries to its destination. The fireworks which marked the beginning now subside. The analogy is pertinent in two different respects, one of which the Pentecostal enthusiasts need especially to remember and the other of which the ecumenically minded must not overlook. On the one hand, the outburst of power is of no importance except as it is channeled to significant continuous uses. On the other hand, all the organizational channels are so much useless paraphernalia without the power of which the fireworks were the evidence.

On both sides, there is always the danger of oversimplification by looking at only one aspect of the total picture. Such an oversimplification is involved in the tendency to think of order and freedom, of organized structure and the spirit, as antithetical. But this is certainly not the New Testament way of viewing the matter. In the New Testament, the Holy Spirit is the dynamic source of power, but the Holy Spirit is not ordinarily given to the indi-

[18] *Op. cit.*, pp. 100–101.

vidual in isolation. It is given to, and works through, the Christian community; and community always means some kind of order. Especially in the thought of St. Paul, the Spirit is not merely something of which an individual has a temporary experience but is "the abiding and indwelling principle of life in a fellowship."[19]

The first of the Pentecostal bodies to become seriously interested in the ecumenical movement is the Pentecostal Church of Chile. Its application for membership in the World Council comes before the next Assembly in New Delhi. In general, however, there are still so few points of personal contact between these groups and the member denominations of the World Council that they know very little of each other.[20]

It is easy to point out the shortcomings of the Pentecostals and even to be patronizing toward their exuberant emotionalism, their lack of Christian social emphasis, and their inadequate appreciation of the church as a historic institution in the world. If we are tempted to such attitudes we may well heed Henry P. Van Dusen's reminder that "Peter and Barnabas and Paul might find themselves more at home in a Holiness service or a Pentecostal revival than in the formalized and sophisticated worship of other Churches." What is called for today is a patient effort to understand why the so-called sects appeal to so many people from whom the older churches evoke slight response.

At the risk of too sweeping generalization, we may perhaps say that the new bodies are lopsided rather than wrong. The almost fantastic preoccupation of some of them with spiritual healing, for example, or with the Second Coming of Christ, shows a lack of balance more than a lack of truth. If such things are over-

[19] *Op. cit.*, p. 115.
[20] Happily, there are exceptions to this generalization. David J. du Plessis, for example, a trusted leader in the Assemblies of God and an important official in all three of the world Pentecostal conferences, attended the Evanston Assembly of the World Council in 1954 and the meeting of the International Missionary Council in Ghana in 1958. He keeps in friendly touch with all ecumenical work. In 1960, he shared in the leadership of a conference on evangelism at the Ecumenical Institute in Bossey. He does not hesitate to call himself an "ecumenical Pentecostalist."

emphasized, it may well be due to their having been under-emphasized in the mainstream churches.

The ecumenical movement, devoted to an understanding of the Christian faith and the Christian Church in their entirety, may well ask itself whether it does not have lessons to learn from the Pentecostals. More particularly, it is timely to raise the question whether a fuller sharing of their accent on the direct and present potency of the Holy Spirit would not be an element of fresh strength. Certainly their evangelistic ardor and missionary vigor may well be coveted by the older churches.

Chapter VI

MORE ROADS THAT DIVERGE

Roman Catholics and the Ecumenical Movement

In the ecumenical movement as it has been taking shape in the last half century the largest body of Christians has no part. The Roman Catholic Church, counting all baptized children, has a world-wide membership of approximately five hundred million. The Protestant bodies, usually defining membership in terms of those who have joined the church by a personal decision, number around two hundred twenty million. The figure for the Eastern Orthodox and the other Eastern Churches like the Coptic and the Abyssinian and the Armenian is especially difficult to estimate on account of the uncertainty as to the numerical strength of the Church of Russia, but perhaps one hundred thirty million is a fair estimate.[1]

The separation between the Roman Catholic Church and the churches of the ecumenical movement is so wide that they are tempted to ignore each other. But for the ecumenical movement

---

[1] All figures of church membership on a world-wide scale represent rough estimates rather than a census. Moreover, the estimates are not really comparable, owing to different definitions of "member." The best available data for the various areas are found in *The World Christian Year Book* (London: World Dominion Press, 1957). See also *Encyclopaedia Britannica, Book of the Year*, 1960.

to do so would be to fail to be ecumenical. Quite apart from the obvious importance of any church of a half billion adherents is the deeper consideration that Roman Catholicism is a great historic form of Christian faith and devotion. We cannot understand the wholeness of Christianity without understanding its Roman expression.

ROMAN VIEW OF UNITY

From its own standpoint, the Roman Catholic Church holds a position with reference to unity that leaves no room for discussion. It regards itself as the only true Church of Christ—One, Holy, Catholic, and Apostolic. It is ruled on earth by the Vicar of Christ, the Roman pontiff, who has his authority as successor to Peter on the throne. The unity of the Church, accordingly, as affirmed again and again and again, depends upon the recognition of this truth and a return to the one divine fold by all who have strayed away like wandering sheep. The general assumption of the Roman Catholic Church has consistently been that in matters of unity it has "everything to teach and nothing to learn."[2] This attitude results in the paradoxical situation that the Church which is the most resolute and tenacious champion of visible unity contributes directly to perpetuating the most serious division.

The "separated brethren" do not all stand on the same level in the eyes of Rome. Some, like the Eastern Orthodox, have sacraments that are accepted as valid, and clergy that are acknowledged to be in the apostolic succession. Others do not. In the case of the Orthodox, all other obstacles to reunion could probably be surmounted if only the Bishop of Rome were to be recognized as supreme. A few groups, once within the Eastern wing of Christendom and now known as "Uniate" Christians, have made their peace with Rome by yielding obedience to the Pope. In these cases, the Roman attitude has been flexible enough to allow them to retain their own Byzantine liturgy and the married priesthood. In the case of bodies which, as viewed by Rome, do not have valid

[2] The phrase is Stephen C. Neill's. See his *Brothers in the Faith* (Nashville: Abingdon Press, 1960), p. 48.

sacraments or clergy in valid orders, the Roman stance is uncompromising.

There is no reason to expect that the Roman Church will retreat from this dogmatic position, but there is evidence that it is now adopting a less aloof attitude toward other Christians. The announcement on January 25, 1959, widely heralded in the press, that Pope John XXIII might "issue an invitation to the separated communities to seek unity" at first created the impression that he might provide for some kind of participation by non-Roman Christians in his proposed "ecumenical council." Although it now appears that no such ecclesiastical summitry is contemplated, the announcement is one of many indications of a growing concern in Rome with the ecumenical movement as it has been developing in recent years. This becomes more clear as one reviews Roman reactions during the last half century to the World Council of Churches and its forerunners.

ATTITUDE TO ECUMENICAL GATHERINGS

In the preparations for the Edinburgh missionary conference of 1910, no attempt was made to include either the Roman Catholic or the Eastern Orthodox Churches. This was natural enough in the case of a conference whose whole attention was focused on missionary expansion. A few years later, when plans for the first World Conference on Faith and Order were getting under way, there was a definite effort to enlist the participation of Roman Catholic and Eastern Orthodox as well as Protestant bodies. Robert H. Gardiner, the secretary of the Commission preparing for the conference, included Cardinal Gasparri, the Secretary of State at the Vatican, in the list of church leaders to whom letters of information about the proposal went as early as 1914. After the interruption of plans due to the First World War, a deputation visited Europe and the Near East to extend invitations to the heads of churches, including Pope Benedict XV. Members of the deputation were graciously received by the Pope but his official answer was an unqualified "No." His written reply declared that "the teaching and practice of the Roman Catholic Church regarding the unity of the visible Church of Christ was well known to everybody and therefore it would not be possible for the Catholic Church to take part in such a congress as the one proposed." He added the hope that "those who take part in it may see the light and become reunited to the visible Head of the Church by whom they will be received with open arms."[3]

This reply is a revealing illustration of the Roman attitude toward other Christian bodies. Holding as a fundamental tenet of faith that its pontiff is Christ's vicegerent on earth, the Roman Church has not been prepared to enter into any consultations which might be interpreted as implying that other churches have anything like an equal status.

The position of Rome was made even more unmistakable by a decree of the Holy Office on the eve of the Lausanne conference on Faith and Order in 1927 forbidding Roman Catholics to attend, and by the subsequent issuance of the encyclical *Mortalium Animos* by Pope Pius XI in 1928. Permitting no compromise of the Roman claim, the encyclical concludes with this take-it-or-leave-it pronouncement:

There is but one way in which the unity of Christians may be fostered, and that is by furthering the return to the one true Church of Christ of those who are separated from it, for from that one true Church they have in the past fallen away.[4]

Although it was thus plain as early as 1919 that the Roman Church would not consider participation in a conference on Faith and Order, there was still the possibility of a different attitude toward ecumenical discussions limited to Christian social responsibility. When the group that initiated plans for the Universal Christian Conference on Life and Work first met in Geneva in 1920, there was a difference of opinion about inviting participation by Rome. The chief figure in the movement, however, Nathan

[3] The full statement is printed in *Faith and Order Pamphlet No. 32*, which is a report of the deputation to Europe and the East.

[4] For a more detailed account of the Roman Catholic position see chap. 15, by Oliver S. Tomkins, in Rouse and Neill, *op cit*. This is a detailed and carefully documented record.

Söderblom, Archbishop of Uppsala, was strongly insistent that all Christian bodies should be included. The outcome of the debate lent support to his view. He therefore undertook, on his own responsibility and in conjunction with the other Scandinavian Lutheran primates, to ascertain the possibility of a favorable response from the Roman Church.

In a letter to the Pope in February, 1921, Archbishop Söderblom and his colleagues laid emphasis on the principle that the proposal for the Stockholm conference did not concern matters of dogma or ritual but was centered wholly upon common endeavors in fields of social and ethical action. The reply from Cardinal Gasparri conveyed the gratitude of His Holiness for the letter, but was silent on the matter of the proposed conference. Archbishop Söderblom therefore had to report to the committee on arrangements in the summer of 1922 that the situation did "not warrant further action." The negative position of Rome was paralleled by what happened in Great Britain in connection with a national Conference on Christian Politics, Economics, and Citizenship. In the early stages of preparation for it, in the months following the First World War, Roman Catholics had participated fully and freely, but they withdrew before the conference took place in 1924.[5]

The attitude of Rome toward both the Life and Work and the Faith and Order conferences, followed by the encyclical *Mortalium Animos*, discouraged further approaches by leaders in any phase of the ecumenical movement. In the studies leading up to the second Life and Work conference, however, held at Oxford in 1937 on the theme "Church, Community, and State," a few Roman Catholic scholars gave a modicum of personal and unofficial co-operation. Christopher Dawson, for example, distinguished British layman, wrote an article on "The Kingdom of God and History" for a preparatory volume. A group of Roman Catholic scholars on the Continent published a volume which dealt

[5] For a fully documented account of Archbishop Söderblom's concern and the Roman Catholic attitude see chap. 11, by Nils Karlström, in Rouse and Neill, *op. cit.*

from their angle with the issues that the Oxford conference was to discuss.[6] At the conference there was no Roman Catholic participation, but a few informal observers attended some of the public sessions.

A year before the second conference on Faith and Order was held at Edinburgh, the Archbishop of York (William Temple) as chairman wrote to the Roman Catholic Archbishop of the area saying that the original invitation to participate in Faith and Order discussions, which had been declined by Rome in 1919, "still stands as part of the whole programme and intention of our movement." Archbishop Temple also added that "if your Grace thinks well to convey this intimation to the Holy See we should be most happy." The reply from the Roman Catholic Archbishop expressed the judgment that "it will be better for me not to co-operate actively in the conference."[7] Five Roman Catholics came to the conference as personal observers, but without participating in any way.

ROME AND THE WORLD COUNCIL

When the Provisional Committee for the World Council of Churches was created and had framed a constitution for submission to the churches, its chairman—again Archbishop Temple—was authorized to communicate information about the plan to the Church of Rome. In February, 1939, he wrote to the Cardinal Secretary of State suggesting that although it was clear that the Roman Catholic Church "would not desire to be formally associated with the Council," it "may be permissible to exchange information . . . on matters of common interest." The letter also expressed the hope that representatives of the Council might have the opportunity "from time to time of unofficial consultation with Roman Catholic theologians and scholars." In reply, the Apostolic

---

[6] Published in German, the volume was entitled *Die Kirche Christi, Grundfragen der Menschen—bildung und Weltgestaltung.* Otto Iserland (ed.), (Einseideln and Cologne, n. d.).

[7] The correspondence is printed in Leonard Hodgson (ed.), *The Second World Conference on Faith and Order* (London: The Macmillan Company, 1938).

Delegate in Great Britain wrote that there would be no obstacle to confidential exchanges of information and opinion.[8]

As the time for the official launching of the World Council drew near, the Provisional Committee authorized an invitation to "a few individual Roman Catholics to attend the assembly as unofficial observers." Several months before it met at Amsterdam, ten Roman Catholics, all of whom had expressed an interest in the ecumenical movement, were invited as individuals. The Holy See, however, did not grant them permission to attend. Instead a *Monitum (Cum Compertum)* was issued on June 5, 1948, which reminded the faithful that canon law did not allow "mixed meetings" without previous permission by the Holy See. As a result, the only Roman Catholics at the Assembly were representatives of the press.

While the Assembly was in session in Amsterdam, the Roman Catholic bishops of the Netherlands issued a pastoral letter explaining why the Roman Church could have no part in it, but urging priests and people to pray for those taking part and for all "who lovingly seek for unity, who truly follow Christ and live in His love and who, although they are separated from Christ's flock, yet look to the Church, be it often unconsciously, as the only haven of salvation."[9]

In the year following the Amsterdam Assembly (1949), an "Instruction to Local Ordinaries" entitled *Ecclesia Catholica*, was issued by the Holy Office in Rome defining its official position as of the present time. While intimating no possibility of union except through submission to Rome, the document lays down conditions under which the faithful may be permitted to have a limited participation in "mixed meetings" on "matters of faith and morals." There is to be no such participation "without the previous sanction of the competent ecclesiastical authority." In the case

[8] The exchange of correspondence is given in full in G. K. A. Bell, *Documents of Christian Unity*, 3rd series (London: Oxford University Press, 1948), pp. 298–299.

[9] For a more detailed account of Roman Catholic attitude and action with reference to the Amsterdam Assembly, see *Ecumenical Review*, Vol. I, No. 2, pp. 797 ff.

of local conferences, the authority is the bishop; in the case of interdiocesan or international conferences, the Holy Office. In "sacred rites," the only permissible measure of participation is joining in the Lord's Prayer, or "some other prayer approved by the Catholic Church," at the beginning or end of meetings. The document was welcomed by ecumenically minded Roman Catholics as making possible some measure of contact with their "separated brethren."

At the third World Conference on Faith and Order, held in Lund in 1952, there were four observers who had been designated by the Vicar Apostolic in Scandinavia after authorization by the Holy Office. This was the first time the Church of Rome had, by due ecclesiastical authority, appointed observers at a gathering of the kind which we call ecumenical. Five years later, when the North American Study Conference on Faith and Order was held in Oberlin, Ohio (1957), two distinguished Roman Catholics, Father Gustave Weigel, S.J., professor in the Jesuit College at Woodstock, Maryland, and Father John B. Sheerin, editor of the *Catholic World*, journal of the Paulist Fathers, were authorized, through the appropriate hierarchical channels, to attend as unofficial observers. They were present at all sessions and occasionally contributed informally to the discussion in the sectional meetings.

In the summer of 1960, two Roman Catholic observers attended the meeting of the World Council's Central Committee at St. Andrews, Scotland, as well as the sessions of the Faith and Order Commission. One of them was Msgr. J. F. M. Willebrands of the Netherlands, who is the secretary of the newly appointed Vatican secretariat for Christian unity. This represents the peak of Roman Catholic approach to ecumenical consultations. It is a conspicuous sign of increasing interest in the ecumenical movement on the part of the Roman Catholic Church.

INTEREST IN ECUMENICAL STUDIES

This is not to be construed as any indication of a softening of the Roman Catholic claim to be the only true Church, or of any relaxing of its dogmatic insistence that the only path to unity is by a

return of the erring children to its bosom. What can fairly be concluded is that Roman Catholic leaders are taking the ecumenical
movement with new seriousness as something of spiritual significance which they need to understand and which they can view
with a kindly eye.

The main evidence of a less aloof attitude is found neither in
official pronouncements nor in unofficial observers but in the volume of current comment and friendly discussion in Roman Catholic circles. This is especially noteworthy in several countries of
Western Europe. When, as a single typical example, an "Ecumenical Assembly of European Youth" was held in Lausanne in 1960,
the bishop of the area, François Charrière, issued a pastoral message commending the theme of the Assembly, "Jesus Christ the
Light of the World," and saying that all sincere efforts for the
reconciliation of Christians are the work of the Holy Spirit.

More important, there are Roman Catholic publications like
Unitas in Rome, *Istina* in France, *Una Sancta* in Germany, and
Irenikon in Belgium, which give continuous attention to ecumenical issues and which reveal much familiarity with the course of
the ecumenical movement. The general tenor of their articles indicates a desire to keep in sympathetic touch with what is taking
place. When criticism is voiced, it is in a courteous and charitable
temper.

In the United States, too, there are increasing signs of Roman
Catholic interest in the churches of the ecumenical movement and
of an attitude toward them that is less rigid. Such a trend becomes
evident to anyone who reads regularly the Jesuit journal *America*,
the lay Roman Catholic magazine the *Commonweal*, or the more
limited *Cross Currents*, a quarterly presentation of articles of basic
theological significance. From time to time *Cross Currents* reprints
important materials by Protestant and Eastern Orthodox scholars
as a contribution to mutual understanding. Those who have
known Roman Catholic journalism only through some of the more
rasping diocesan papers will be happily surprised to see how very
different it can be.

There are also substantial volumes by Roman Catholic authors which reflect a similar attitude toward the ecumenical movement. One of these in America is Father George H. Tavard's *The Catholic Approach to Protestantism*, a vigorous plea for "spiritual emulation" and a "creative peace" between Roman Catholic and Protestant.[10] Another is *The Social Thought of the World Council of Churches* by Father Edward Duff, S.J.[11] In gathering data for the book, he not only made an intensive examination of the studies that the Council has carried on in the socio-ethical field, but also held many personal conversations with its staff in Geneva. His treatment is marked by an admirable objectivity and fairness. Indeed, his book was a more complete analysis of the subject than had come from any Protestant pen up to that time.

It appears, then, that the Roman Catholic Church remains outside the ecumenical movement, but not altogether outside the ecumenical conversation now going on throughout the Christian world. It may be unrealistic to assume that this will have any marked effect on ecclesiastical policy, but we can at least be grateful if Roman Catholics and Protestants can face their differences, radical as they are, as Christian brethren rather than as participants in a "cold war." They have far more in common with each other than either group has with those who reject the Lordship of Christ—and they ought to make this obvious to the world.

PRAYER FOR UNITY

The most gratifying manifestation of the new mood is the increasing disposition of Roman Catholics to join with "separated brethren" in a concrete movement of prayer for unity. The original initiative came largely from an ecumenically minded Roman Catholic, the Abbé Paul Couturier, in the diocese of Lyons, France. Beginning in the nineteen-thirties, with encouragement from the Archbishop of Lyons, he issued an annual "Call to Prayer," which did not specify a return to Rome, but "the visible unity of all Christians such as Christ wishes and through the means which He will choose." Since the death of the Abbé, the call has

[10] New York: Harper & Brothers, 1955.
[11] New York: Association Press, 1956.

been continued by Father Pierre Michalon. The period of prayer, January 18-25, was fixed by the consideration that in Roman Catholic circles there was already a "Chair of Unity Octave" at this time, extending from the Feast of St. Peter's Chair to the Feast of the Conversion of St. Paul. In 1941, the Faith and Order movement, which had for twenty years been urging prayer for unity during the week ending on Whitsunday, shifted the date to coincide with the Abbé Couturier's call. The week of prayer is not promoted through joint meetings, but Christians of all the different ecclesiastical backgrounds are encouraged to use the forms that they find most meaningful and to do so in the consciousness that they are sharing in a wide concert of intercession for the unity of the family of Christ.

The number of those who observe this annual week of prayer in the spirit which the Abbé Couturier urged may be fairly small. In America, the observance of the Chair of Unity Octave, as promoted by the Franciscan Friars of the Atonement, has a very different character. It is based upon an out-and-out appeal for the conversion of all non-Roman Christians to Rome. Instead of prayer for the unity of the church as Christ wills it, there is prayer for unity as defined by Rome. This divergence is a revealing illustration of the gravity of the problem of unity between Roman Catholics and other Christians. So long as a church takes an attitude toward unity which even in prayer would mean for all other communions a repudiation of their own history, the price of reunion will always be higher than they can pay.

Although there is no prospect that the Roman Catholic Church will abandon its claim to exclusive authority or officially acknowledge other churches as churches, there is ground for hope that it may become less isolationist in its relationships. It is entirely possible that in matters which do not directly involve its dogmatic interpretation of the faith, an increasing measure of co-operation with other bodies of Christians may be permitted. Two areas may be especially open to such a development.

The first is the area of study. There are already more points of contact between Protestant and Roman Catholic scholars than most people in either group realize. They are reading each other's books. To some extent, they are beginning to share in common discussions. This is much more true in some of the European countries than in America.

Another area in which growing collaboration may be feasible is that of Christian social ethics and humanitarian service. It may be only on rare occasions that such projects will have as much of an official aura as the remarkable—and too much forgotten—joint inquiry into the twelve-hour day in the steel industry in 1923, mentioned earlier, in which staff members of the Federal Council of Churches and the National Catholic Welfare Conference shared. But informal consultation is always possible and may be genuinely significant. If combined efforts are not practicable, parallel efforts may be, and may result in a measure of common Christian witness. An important current example of this is the way in which harmonious policies for the resettlement of refugees have been developed through occasional consultations between representatives of the World Council of Churches and of Roman Catholic agencies. In America, an especially happy example is "One Great Hour of Sharing," initiated by Church World Service, which includes not only Protestants and Roman Catholics but also Jews in simultaneous appeals to the public in behalf of the suffering in all parts of the world. The number of such illustrations is likely to increase.

A MORE IRENIC CLIMATE

That Roman Catholics and Protestants have responsibilities for each other as sharers in the Christian heritage cannot be too strongly insisted. The first aspect of that responsibility, surely, is to make a more patient effort to understand each other. That is not easy. Both Roman Catholicism and Protestantism are too complex to be quickly comprehended. Too long has each been content to go its separate way. In most communities, Roman Catholic priest and Protestant minister have had no more than a nodding acquaintance—if as much as that. Their only contacts have been such casual ones as come from finding themselves together at a civic gathering or a Rotary Club luncheon. And most of what they have read about each other's faith and practice has been too polemical to be conducive to a desire for fuller acquaintance.

As a result, most Protestants are unaware of current developments in Roman Catholicism which afford ground for hope that there may be more of a common mind at certain points in years ahead. One of the most pregnant of these is the heightened interest in the Bible—almost a rediscovery of the Bible—among Roman Catholics. A papal encyclical of 1943, *Divino afflante Spiritu*, encouraged the reading of the Bible by lay people. New translations of the Scriptures have appeared under Roman Catholic auspices in several lands. The educational institutions of the Church have expanded their teaching of the Bible. The Catholic Biblical Association of America and the Society of Biblical Literature and Exegesis (Protestant) have recently decided to send delegates to each other's annual meetings. At Oxford, a group interested in New Testament studies, presided over by the Archbishop of York, has included a Roman Catholic archbishop.

It remains true, of course, that the authority of Scripture for the Roman Church is linked with the authority of tradition and that both Scripture and tradition are interpreted by the hierarchy. Pope Pius XII could thus in 1950 proclaim the dogma of the Assumption of the Virgin Mary "both in body and soul" into heaven even though both the Bible and the tradition of the earliest Christian centuries are entirely silent on the subject. Nevertheless, the increased reading and study of the Bible by Roman Catholics is something that Protestants can gratefully recognize as affording the possibility of a stronger bond between them.

Along with the revived interest in the Scriptures there is a seminal development in Roman Catholicism that is called "liturgical revival." To be ignorant of this is to miss a very important trend. Not merely a movement for the revision of liturgical forms, it involves an effort to promote a deepened understanding of the meaning of worship for the Christian community. It emphasizes an informed participation of the laity in the liturgy of the mass as the central act of worship, in contrast with secondary and more individualistic expressions of piety, such as those associated with rosaries and novenas. The movement further stresses Christian instruction through preaching and the interpretation of the liturgical year. There is also a burgeoning interest in contemporary art and architecture in the service of the Roman Church. In Switzerland or France, for example, one can see today Roman Catholic churches that are impressive for their simplicity and the absence of the cluttering objects that often strike a visitor unfavorably.

Many American Protestants do not yet seem aware how the great change in their cultural situation is affecting the religious patterns. They are accustomed to think of American culture as Protestant—as, indeed, it conspicuously has been in origin and history. The national ethos has been powerfully influenced by the Protestant tradition. Until the twentieth century, non-Protestant contributions were minor enough to seem almost negligible. As recently as 1927, a discerning French observer, André Siegfried, could even say that Protestanism was America's "only national religion."[12] To the Protestant, America has seemed peculiarly his country and Catholicism has appeared like an alien intruder. American Catholics, viewed at best with a patronizing air and at worst with suspicious hostility, felt themselves a beleaguered minority and tended to develop a ghetto mentality. In defense of their own inheritance, they tended to shut themselves off from much association with powerful neighbors.[13]

The American scene in the nineteen-sixties stands in sharp contrast with this earlier picture. As a result of the successive waves of immigrants and their assimilation to American standards, the non-Protestant elements are no longer slight either in numerical terms or in participation in the national life. There has been a gradual transition from a dominantly Protestant to a pluralistic culture. By and large, however, neither Protestant nor Catholic is fully conscious of the changed attitude toward each

[12] *America Comes of Age* (New York: Harcourt, Brace and Company, 1927), p. 33.
[13] For a Roman Catholic sociologist's interpretation of this situation and of the change that has now taken place, see Thomas F. O'Dea, "The New America," *Pulpit Digest*, November, 1959.

other which the sociological changes call for. The Roman
Catholic still tends to maintain the old aloofness in the religious
world, even though deeply immersed in all the other aspects
of community life. The Protestant has not yet entirely lost
his old feeling that Roman Catholic priests and nuns are to be
viewed with some distrust as agents of a foreign ecclesiastical
power.

In large, urban, industrialized areas, which are more and
more the centers of cultural influence, Roman Catholics may
even be a majority today. Certainly, no one could describe the
culture of New York or Boston or Philadelphia as Protestant.
Where Roman Catholics are weak in numbers they may be
relatively strong in other ways as a result of their organizational
cohesion and centralized authority, in contrast with the divided
institutional loyalties of Protestants. There is no longer any real
reason either for Roman Catholic defensiveness or for Protestant
assumption of cultural domination. What is needed as a corrective
on both sides is a frank and continuous give-and-take of conversation—"a dialogue," to use the term that has become almost a cliché
—between the two groups in an atmosphere of common concern
for Christian faith and Christian witness in an increasingly
secularized society.

CONFLICTING VIEWS OF AUTHORITY

When everything else that is pertinent to the issues between
Roman Catholic and Protestant has been said, it is the question
of authority that marks the ultimate dividing line. Not that
Protestantism rejects the idea of authority. The thoughtful
Protestant knows himself to be under the authority of the Word
of God as spoken through Jesus Christ. But he does reject the
idea that the exercise of this divine authority can be delegated
to any human instrumentality. "The Protestant principle," as
Paul Tillich calls it, is that every historical movement, every
human achievement, every institutional development, always
stands under the judgment of the God who has revealed His will
in Jesus Christ. The Roman Catholic position, however, is that

there is one tremendous exception, namely, the Church, since the Bishop of Rome as Vicar of Christ on earth exercises authority for Him in matters of faith and morals. To the Protestant, this claim can only mean that the Roman Catholic Church stands under no authority except itself. It is at this point that Roman Catholic and Protestant come to the decisive parting of the ways.

To this fundamental cleavage, the chief tensions between Roman Catholic and Protestant, even in the social and civic realm, can be traced. In such a concrete case as birth control, for example, no problem arises from the Roman Church's prescribing the duty of its own members. The difficulty comes when the Church, on the premise of its absolute authority in matters of faith and morals, claims the right to impose its position on others—by trying, for instance, to prevent non-Catholic physicians from having a legal right to give contraceptive information to non-Catholics.

The whole vexing issue of religious liberty in situations in which Roman Catholicism is dominant is likewise rooted in the doctrine of authority. If it be granted that the Roman Church is the consolidated center of Christ's authority on earth, it would follow that it has the right to decide what forms of Christian teaching and practice may be allowed. None of the assurances which Roman Catholic spokesmen give in trying to allay Protestant fears comes to terms with this crucial point. They reasonably argue that in a democratic society like the American, their Church would never follow the procedures which have been deemed appropriate in a Catholic state like Spain, but the Achilles' heel in the argument remains. For if the Roman Church really possessed the authority which it claims for itself, it would always be justified, whenever circumstances were right, in maintaining exclusive prerogatives for itself as the only true Church. For the American political scene, the issue is whether Paul Tillich is right when he says that "it is one of the paradoxes of Protestantism in this country that it must be tolerant toward those who by their very nature must destroy tolerance at the moment when the tolerant processes of democracy have brought them into power."[14]

CONFLICT OVER RELIGIOUS LIBERTY

Unknown to many Protestants, a significant tension is appearing in the Roman Catholicism of today over its traditional attitude toward religious liberty. Serious questions are being raised by Roman Catholics themselves about the policy of looking to any state to grant a preferred position to their Church. How much influence the new viewpoint will prove to have no one can yet foretell. But it can at least be said that it is being put forward by able theologians who are in good standing in their Church and who publish their conclusions without hindrance from ecclesiastical authority.

A German Jesuit, Father Albert Hartmann, summarizes the present situation by saying that "there is no unanimity on this question in the Catholic world." "One group of theologians," he adds, "may defend the 'Catholic state' as a direct conclusion from the Catholic faith's claim to truth; other theologians may reject it completely." He himself insists that religious liberty is "fully compatible with the principles of the Church" and repudiates the view that the Catholic state should by law prevent the propagation of "error." French Roman Catholics are especially concerned over the issue. Popular lay Catholics like Jacques Maritain defend the concept of religious liberty, and a distinguished French priest, Father Augustin Leonard, concludes: "The only answer which is fully in keeping with the free nature of faith is the promulgation of religious freedom, not as a lesser evil, to be borne out of unwilling tolerance . . . but as a principle, permanently and finally established."[15] It is clear that the Roman Catholic Church might come to a positive at-

[14] *The Theology of Culture: Essays by Paul Tillich* (New York: Oxford University Press, 1959), p. 181.

[15] For the documentation on this and many other Roman Catholic utterances in a similar vein, see the exceedingly valuable study, *Roman Catholicism and Religious Liberty*, by A. F. Carillo de Albornoz (Geneva: World Council of Churches, 1959).

titude in support of religious liberty if it should heed its own best voices.

Father John Courtney Murray, S.J., theologian of Woodstock College, Maryland, and editor of the Jesuit quarterly, *Theological Studies*, has for several years been giving major attention to the Roman Catholic philosophy of church and state. He contends that the traditional position of the Roman Church, which, when it has the power to do so, denies freedom and equality of legal standing to other religious bodies, was formulated before the emergence of a truly democratic state like the United States and therefore needs redefinition. America, he says, is a new kind of political entity, unlike the "confessional state" of Europe. "The starting point," to quote one of his summaries of this trend in Roman Catholic thought, is different, not a "national religious unity to be preserved by the action of the Throne in union with the Altar, but the spiritual unity of the whole man in his concrete and historic reality, to be preserved by the action of the citizen, that is, by his freedom so to direct the processes of government and the institutions of society that they will not disrupt but solidify his spiritual unity."[16]

Over against this new point of view there are, of course, contrary (and more official) voices in the Roman Church. Cardinal Ottaviani, for example, as recently as 1953 vigorously championed the traditional position in a widely quoted address defending the Spanish conception of the Catholic state. An article in *La Civiltà Cattolica* in 1950 was an even more blunt and unqualified reaffirmation of the traditional ideal. This publication of the Society of Jesus in Rome said:

The Roman Catholic Church, convinced, through its divine prerogatives, of being the only true Church, must demand the right to freedom for herself alone, because such a right can only be possessed by truth, never by error. As to other religions, the Church will certainly never draw the sword, but she will require that by legitimate means they shall not be allowed to propagate false doctrine.[17]

[16] *Theological Studies* (Woodstock, Md.: June, 1949).
[17] Extensive citations in support of both sides of the current debate in Roman Catholicism on this subject are given by Carillo de Albornoz, *op. cit.*

This is, of course, a restatement of nineteenth-century papal encyclicals on the subject, such as *Libertas* of Pope Leo XIII, which, as late as 1888, declared that "the state cannot adopt the same attitude to all religions and grant them the same rights without discrimination."

An important impression left on us by this conflict of view is that there is more room for differences in Roman Catholicism over political principles and policies than most Protestants assume. We can hardly help asking, however, who represents the future position of the Roman Church—Father Murray and the French and German scholars who are in accord with him or Cardinal Ottaviani and *La Civiltà Cattolica?* Is the new view merely being tolerated or might it really become official Roman Catholic doctrine? In a church as centralized in its authority as the Roman Catholic, it is unlikely that both positions will exist permanently side by side. Can the papal encyclicals of the nineteenth century be so reinterpreted as to justify a new orientation toward religious liberty? If it be admitted that their judgments about the relation of church and state were conditioned by the historical circumstances of the time, just how much authority do encyclicals have? Can a reinterpretation of them be reconciled with the claim to the infallibility of the Pope? Finally, is there an unbridgeable inconsistency between the theological doctrine that the Roman Church possesses the authority of God and an acknowledgment of complete religious liberty as the right of those who do not accept Rome as an authority?

NEED FOR ECUMENICAL DIALOGUE

In the informal and unofficial dialogue in which Protestants and Roman Catholics need to engage for the sake of growth in mutual understanding, it will be necessary to include fundamental issues of doctrine. The dialogue can best begin at the point of social-ethical concerns, where common ground is more likely to be found, but in the end these issues are rooted in theological convictions that cannot be ignored.

A concrete illustration of what is desirable was the invitation of the Yale Divinity School to Father Gustave Weigel to deliver the Nathaniel Taylor Lectures in 1960 on "The Direction of Current Catholic Theology."[18] He was the first Roman Catholic theologian to appear on this platform. Another illustration was the earlier decision of the Harvard Divinity School to invite Christopher Dawson, distinguished Roman Catholic scholar of Great Britain, to be a visiting member of its faculty. A more localized example of a similar reaching out for better mutual acquaintance was the action of St. Paul's Lutheran Church in Toledo, Ohio, in arranging ecumenical conferences in both 1959 and 1960 which included Roman Catholic participation. On the international level, the Ecumenical Institute at Bossey, near Geneva, has had Roman Catholic guests on several occasions.

It is greatly to be hoped that the rising interest in the ecumenical movement on the part of thoughtful Roman Catholics may lead the hierarchy to encourage the faithful to share in conversations that involve ultimate questions of faith. The very fact that such a dialogue was taking place continuously, as a substitute for the monologues of the past, would help to create the kind of atmosphere in which separated Christians should live together and bear their witness in an unbelieving world. Without compromising their grave differences, they would be testifying that they worship the same God, see Him revealed in the same Christ, use the same Bible, and seek to live by the standards of the same Lord.

When the National Council of the Churches of Christ in the U.S.A. met in San Francisco in December, 1960, the *Monitor*, official publication of the Roman Catholic archdiocese, carried an editorial welcoming the delegates. It said in part: "The Council's overarching hope is Christian unity. The sincerity and humility of its representatives are transparently clear. Their growing desire for unity can only be attributed to the action of the Holy Spirit." The editorial went on to urge Roman Catholics to "avail themselves of the literature of ecumenism"

[18] Included in his *Catholic Theology in Dialogue* (New York: Harper & Brothers, 1961).

Chapter VII

THE ROAD AHEAD

Where Local and Ecumenical Meet

In spite of the phenomenal rise of the ecumenical movement, it is still only a marginal concern in most congregations. Church leaders are officially committed to it. By and large, pastors and thoughtful laymen wish it well. But they are all preoccupied with their own immediate interests. Local and denominational activities fully occupy the center of the stage, and ecumenical responsibility is left on the outer edges.

A comment which Bishop Angus Dun made about the Protestant Episcopal Church in the United States after the first Assembly of the World Council is true of the churches generally. He pointed out that the Episcopalian delegates returned from Amsterdam with so much enthusiasm that a session of the General Convention of the church was devoted to the ecumenical movement. The presentations were stirring. The response was cordial. And then the Convention settled down to what it regarded as "its own business" and soon forgot any continuing ecumenical concern. As Bishop Dun pointedly remarked, "There was an ecumenical interest but it was a sideshow, not under the main tent."

If this tempts us to be discouraged about the future, we should remind ourselves that there have been other great Christian responsibilities which began as "sideshows" but are now "under the main tent." The missionary obligation to proclaim the gospel to all the world was once left to zealous individuals and voluntary societies. But the time came when a church that had no part in the missionary movement was looked upon as deficient in its essential life. The Christian education of children, too, was once hardly more than a sideshow, but the day came when a congregation that did not assume full oversight of a church school was thought of as failing in its duty.

The most serious weakness of the ecumenical movement today is that it is generally regarded as the responsibility of a few national leaders in each denomination and a few interdenominational executives. Most pastors and laymen, even though they believe it to be important, assume that the ecumenical movement lies outside the province of their parishes. They may even dismiss it from their minds as something that concerns only the "ecclesiastical Rover Boys," as someone has dubbed them, who like to go to national and international assemblies, and have expense accounts that permit them to do so.

As long as this point of view prevails, the ecumenical movement will be lame and halt. The next stage ahead is that of making it thoroughly at home in the local community. Progress will take place far less through what is done in any "summit conference" of the National Council or the World Council, or even in offices of denominational boards, than through what happens in the communities where Christian people live together as neighbors. The front line of advance is where witnessing and worshiping congregations of different traditions exist side by side. Until they see the ecumenical movement in terms of the difference it makes in their own attitudes, programs, and relationships, it will have an inevitable aspect of unreality. As things now stand, there is a grievous disparity between the unity in Christ which we profess in ecumenical meetings and the complacent separateness of most congregations on any Main Street in the nation.

THE ECUMENICAL CONGREGATION

The crux of ecumenical advance is an even more personalized matter than the relation between congregations in the same community. The decisive question is what happens *within* each congregation and, finally, in the minds and hearts of the individual members. It is here that the local and ecumenical must meet. It is here that the ecumenical must become local and the local become ecumenical.

It has become almost trite to say that the ecumenical movement must be "carried down to the grass roots." This way of describing the matter is unfortunate. It implies two misconceptions. One is that whatever is ecumenical has to do with some over-all organization at "the top" and needs only to be understood at the so-called "lower levels." The truth, however, is that the ecumenical church *is* just the local church in its own true character as an integral unit of the whole People of God throughout the world. The other misconception is that our ecumenical problems will be solved if only the knowledge of the church in its world-wide extension and its interdenominational connections, now comprehended by many national leaders, can be communicated to all congregations. However needed this may be, the fundamental problem is not information but active commitment to the total mission of the church of Christ in the world.

The basic unit in the church, of whatever denominational polity, is always the congregation. It is hardly possible to emphasize this too much. Most people do not realize that the congregation, as a gathered fellowship meeting regularly face to face, personally sharing in a common experience and expressing that experience in daily relationships with one another, is unique. The idea that it is a feature of all religions is entirely mistaken. The Jewish synagogue affords a parallel to the Christian congregation, but Hinduism, Buddhism, Islam, Confucianism, Taoism, Shintoism, although they have sacred scriptures, priests, spiritual disciplines, and places of prayer, do not have a congregation as a local household of faith and love. Their characteristic experience is that of the individual at an altar or a shrine rather than that of a continuing social group with a distinctive kind of fellowship.

How far the fellowship in most local churches falls below what the New Testament means by *koinonia!* What is now called Christian fellowship is often little more than the social chumminess of having a gracious time with the kind of people one likes. The *koinonia* of Acts and of the Epistles means sharing in a common relation to Christ. It is an experience of a new depth of community derived from an awareness of the corporate indwelling of Christ in His people. As Dietrich Bonhöffer puts it, "Our community with one another consists solely in what Christ has done to both of us."[1] This may mean having fellowship in the church with people with whom, on the level of merely human agreeableness, we might prefer not to have any association at all. There is a vast difference between the community of reconciliation which the New Testament describes and the community of congeniality found in the average church building.

Whenever a congregation really sees itself as a unit in the universal Church, in vital relation with the whole Body of Christ and participating in His mission to the world, a necessary foundation-stone of the ecumenical movement has been laid. The antithesis of the ecumenical and the local then no longer exists. The local and the ecumenical are one.

Of course, the perspective of those who are dealing directly with the world-wide problems of the People of God will always be different from the perspective of those who are dealing with the nearby problems of particular persons in a particular place. Each viewpoint is valid if it is organically related to the other. Neither is adequate if it stands alone. Our difficulty arises when either viewpoint shuts out the other. And this is what all too often happens.

[1] *Life Together*, trans. by John W. Doberstein (New York: Harper & Brothers, 1954), p. 25.

DIVERGENT PERSPECTIVES

A little parable illustrative of this truth is afforded by an incident related by Professor Bela Vasady at the end of the Second World War. With great difficulty he made his way from his native Hungary to Geneva to renew his contacts as a member of the Provisional Committee for the World Council of Churches. When he had the mishap of breaking his spectacles, his ecumenical colleagues insisted on providing him with new ones. They were bifocals. He often spoke of them as his "ecumenical" glasses and used them as a symbol of the kind of vision that is required in the church. It is, he said, a bifocal vision, which can see both the near-at-hand and the distant and keep a Christian in right relation to both.

As things stand now, the local and the ecumenical tend to compete with each other. On the one hand, there are ecumenists who are so stirred by the crises of the church in its encounter with the world at large that they have no eyes for what the church is doing in their own town. They do not escape the pitfall into which Charles Dickens pictured Mrs. Jellyby as falling. Her concern for the natives of Borrioboola-Gha was so intense that she quite forgot and neglected her son Peepy! Likewise, the ecumenist may become so absorbed in the conflict of the church with the totalitarian state in East Germany, the precarious situation of the church in revolutionary China, and the anguish of the church over apartheid in South Africa that he loses close contact with the parish church in its unspectacular but indispensable ministry of worship, pastoral service and counseling, and Christian nurture for a face-to-face group of individuals.

On the other hand, many a pastor is so absorbed in ministering to the intimate, personal needs of individuals in his congregation that he does little or nothing to lead them into a sense of social responsibility and world mission. As a result, they go on thinking of the church, with introverted and self-centered satisfaction, only in connection with the way in which it serves them and their families. It would hardly be an exaggeration to say that ninety per cent of the energy of most churches— whether in terms of finance or spiritual concern—is poured into the private and domestic interests of the members. The parish lives for itself rather than for the community or the world.

The gap between the ecumenical perspective and the parish perspective appears most starkly in a church in any of our comfortable suburbs. It is eminently successful according to all conventional standards. It is growing in numbers. Its people are agreeable friends. It has a beautiful edifice. Its preaching and its music give refreshment of spirit to men and women living under heavy strain. It provides pastoral care for the sick and troubled. It helps children grow up with at least a nodding acquaintance with the Bible. It draws young people into the circle of those who continue the life of the church from generation to generation. And it is easy for the ecumenical enthusiast to lose sight of how basic all this is.

But what is this church doing to help its members understand their role as Christians in the world? All too often its conception of parish ministry and pastoral care includes no responsibility for them in their relation to issues of the most desperate urgency for the life of mankind. It is not stirring them to confront the racial tensions of today with the mind of Christ. It is not helping them face the moral crisis involved in the use of nuclear energy. It is not making them sensitive to the sub-Christian level of much of our economic and industrial life. It is raising no disturbing question as to what Christian stewardship means for the relationship of the richest nation in the world to economically underdeveloped peoples. It is not developing an awareness of the new kind of missionary strategy that is called for as young churches emerge in Asia and Africa.

To put it bluntly, many a local church is giving its members only what they consciously want. It is not disturbing them by thoughts of their Christian responsibility in relation to the world. We shall not make a decisive advance in the ecumenical movement until such a church begins to see itself not merely as a haven of comfort and peace but as a base of Christian witness and mission to the world.

There is a humorous but revealing story about a rancher who owned a large slice of Texas and who wanted to have on it everything that was necessary for a completely pleasant community. He built a school and a library, then a recreation center and an inn. Desiring to fill the only remaining lack, he selected the best site on the ranch for a chapel and spared no expense in erecting it. A visitor to the beautiful little building inquired, "Do you belong to this church, Mr. Rancher?" "Why, no, ma'am," he replied, "this church belongs to me!" The story reflects the way too many people feel. As long as the congregation regards the church as "our" church, or the minister thinks of it as "my" church, just so long the ecumenical movement will make no significant advance. There must first be a deeper sense that the church belongs not to us but to Christ, and that it is His purpose, not our own interests and preferences, that determines what it is to be and do.

LOCAL EMBODIMENT OF THE WHOLE

A local church which conceives its function to be entirely that of ministering to the conscious desires and concerns of its members tends to look on everything ecumenical as an extra, not as a normal aspect of its own life as a church. It would doubtless be greatly surprised to be told that in failing to be ecumenical it is really failing to be the Church of Christ.

Yet the truth, according to the New Testament, is that every local church has its existence only by being the embodiment of the whole church in that particular place. As Ernest F. Scott summarizes, "From the outset the Church was understood universally." For St. Paul, accordingly, the antithesis between ecumenical and local never appears. This is for the simple reason that he sees every congregation as representing the one Church of God. He calls each little Christian community not *a* church but "*the* church"—as, for example, in his salutation to "the Church of God which is in Corinth." It was the Body of Christ in a specified place, carrying on there His redemptive mission to the world. It had no real existence otherwise. It was God's Church, not an organization with which Corinthians might do as they pleased. He rebukes any such presumptuousness on their part by asking sharply, "Did God's message start from you Corinthians? Or are you the only people it has reached?"[2]

Thus, for St. Paul, the universality and the unity of the church were not achieved by any process of adding local churches together. The essential truth was just the opposite. The universality and the unity had been determined by the fact of one Lord before any congregation had been organized. The fundamental thing was that there is one Body because there is "one God and Father of us all, who is above all, through all and in all." So the crucial New Testament test for every local church is whether it is functioning in such a way that the one universal Church "comes alive" for the people in that community. If it does, there is no lack of concord between local and ecumenical.

When a local church becomes vividly conscious of itself as a unit in a universal fellowship, a new dimension is added to the meaning of church membership. The member now sees that through his congregation he belongs to a community that is not merely local, not merely American, not merely Western, but world-wide. In fact, there is no other voluntary association to which he can belong that unites him with people of so many different cultures and nations. In a world that seems to be more and more breaking apart, he is a link in a chain of fellowship that binds people together around the globe at the deepest level of their lives. In the third century, when the Roman Empire was disintegrating, the Epistle to Diognetus dared to say that "Christians hold the world together." It is something like this vision of the possible role of the Christian community that every congregation in the twentieth century needs to gain.

[2] I Cor. 14:36 (Edgar J. Goodspeed, *The Bible*, An American Translation).

As a concrete illustration of the need for the local and the ecumenical thus to interpenetrate and give meaning to each other, consider the present situation with reference to racial segregation. The church in its ecumenical expression is unequivocally on record as holding that segregation is indefensible on Christian grounds. Both denominational and interdenominational bodies, both National and World Councils, have defined a forthright position. Yet what inch-slow progress churches in local communities make in dealing with the issue in their own life!

RACIAL ISSUES: LOCAL AND UNIVERSAL

It is easy, in consequence, either to become scornful of the ecumenical statements on race as unrealistic and even hypocritical or to condemn the local attitude as unenlightened and benighted. Neither reaction would be justified. The reason for the paradoxical situation is that the racial problem itself appears different when approached from exclusively the ecumenical or the local angle.

When representatives of the churches are in an ecumenical setting, they are conscious of realities which any local church easily forgets: namely, that the church is a world-wide community, that it draws its members from every race and culture, that two-thirds of the people of the world are not white, that the witness to the Christian gospel and the Christian fellowship is fatally crippled by a congregation that insists on segregation. From an ecumenical standpoint, all this is so crystal-clear that only the blindest could miss it. Segregation in a church appears in its true light as climactic evidence that it is failing to be the Christian *koinonia*.

In the perspective of the local church, however, the practical problems of the immediate situation may be very complex. Here there are social pressures which were not felt in the ecumenical gathering—the kind of pressures that arise, for example, from different levels of economic status between the races and accordingly of educational and cultural development. It is hardly surprising if local churches feel that the Church Ecumenical has not taken their difficulties into account and makes its generalizations without sufficient attention to the diverse and complicated conditions to which they are to be applied.

Yet how desperately a local church needs the ecumenical corrective of the myopic vision that cannot reach beyond its own narrow circle! The very fact that it is subjected to powerful social and cultural pressures means that it may not even be aware how sub-Christian or even anti-Christian its attitude is. Except for an involvement in the ecumenical movement, it may never realize how stultifying it is to send missionaries to Africa to bring Negroes into the Christian fellowship and at the same time close the doors to Christian fellowship with them in its own community. Any Christian solution of the national and international problems of race depends on the degree to which the ecumenical viewpoint, which thinks of the church in its wholeness in relation to the world in its wholeness, wins its way in the local church.

An instructive illustration of the way in which the ecumenical perspective bears on a local situation appears in what happened in one congregation during a crisis over desegregation in the schools. When, at one stage, the authorities in Front Royal, Virginia, decided to close public schools rather than to permit Negro and white children to be in the same classrooms, the First Baptist Church was requested to make its facilities available for a private school. By a divided vote the congregation acceded to the request, but the minister, as a result of his ecumenical contacts, made a discerning statement in opposition. He said in part:

To many the issue is a simple one: namely, a compassionate concern to remove our youth from the streets and to provide education for them during an emergency period. The situation, however, is far from this simple. . . . My understanding of the Gospel and of the Church as a fellowship rising above the accidents of race, class, and nationality leads me to dissent. . . . Our Lord has commissioned us to go unto the uttermost part of the earth and to preach the Gospel. . . . If we fail here to make plain that the Gospel is a universal Gospel, whose temple is a "House of Prayer for all people," we will weaken our witness and undercut our mission as a Church.[3]

Another example of an impact of ecumenical perspective upon a local situation comes from the struggle over apartheid in South Africa. The Dutch Reformed Church there has been closely identified with governmental officialdom and therefore hesitant to take any critical position. It has been, however, a member of the World Council of Churches, and this has meant an exposure to the views of Christian bodies in other lands. When the moderator of the church returned from the Evanston Assembly in 1954, he reported that its statement on race involved "a clear and strong condemnation of our conceptions and practice" with regard to segregation. He added that when the delegates of the Dutch Reformed Church of South Africa had failed to secure modification of the statement, they had seriously discussed whether they should withdraw from the Council. He then concluded with this comment as to why they had not done so:

Our place is inside the community of the faithful and not outside it. Our membership in the World Council of Churches . . . submits us to a challenge from a wider circle and forces us to the beneficial discipline of constantly examining ourselves and testing ourselves, our opinions and our baffling problems, by the word of God. . . . We must be ready to come together in Christian tolerance and forbearance with other believers, not only to say what we have to say but to listen when others speak and to consider whether in their words we do not, by any chance, hear the word of God.[4]

Even though the church subsequently withdrew from the World Council, the ecumenical experience has had an influence of which the last has not yet been heard. A new mood of self-examination has entered into the local scene.

[3] Paul L. Stagg, *Pulpit Digest*, January, 1959.
[4] Minutes of Executive Committee of World Council of Churches, February 7-11, 1955, in Geneva. Appendix A.

Concrete Steps Locally

If a congregation wants to become truly a local embodiment of the Church Ecumenical, there are concrete steps in this direction which it can take at once and which do not involve waiting for any denominational decision or any change in organizational structures.

As a first thing, the minister could make it clear that when one joins the church he joins not a Lutheran church in Middletown or a Presbyterian church in Jonesville but the whole Church of Christ throughout the world. This would both enrich greatly the significance of membership for the individual and give the ecumenical movement a firmer foundation. Under present conditions, few Christians think of their relation to the church as involving more than a local, or at most a denominational, responsibility. The various liturgical forms for reception of members and most of the courses for communicant classes reveal a distressing paucity of anything that explicitly indicates the world-wide character of the fellowship or participation in a mission to the world.

For another thing, the worship of the church could be more consciously related to the life of the universal fellowship. How many congregations, Sunday after Sunday, pray intelligently for the whole family of Christ? In those that use a regular liturgy, there may be, indeed, a prayer for "the whole state of Christ's Church," but it is open to wonder how much concrete connotation it carries for identifying the worshiper with fellow-Christians around the globe. How many congregations offer frequent intercession for Christians in the most trying contemporary situations—those, for example, who are struggling to preserve the church in China or East Germany? How many congregations ever pray even for parishes of other denominations in their own town? Imaginative intercession for fellow Christians might do more than any other single thing to nourish an ecumenical spirit in the church.

The ecumenical spirit thus voiced in prayer is further nourished as it finds channels of active expression. In a world in which there are vast disparities of material resources, interchurch aid on an interdenominational and international basis is one of the most obvious ways by which any congregation can be consciously ecumenical. The "One Great Hour of Sharing," as projected by Church World Service, affords a special opportunity for thus identifying a parish with the world-wide Christian community.

The hymnal has resources which might be used more ecumenically. Nearly all worshipers are far more ecumenical in song than they are wont to realize. Brief comments on the diverse sources, confessional and national, from which the great hymns of every local church are drawn, would be a simple way of fostering an understanding of the ecumenical character of the church. Many a Protestant layman would be surprised to discover how much he owes to Christians from whom he is sharply separated if he realized that he was refreshing his spiritual life by a Greek Orthodox hymn like "The Day of Resurrection" or a Roman Catholic hymn like "Jesus, Thou Joy of Loving Hearts."

In terms of program, the local Council of Churches is usually the best channel of connection with ecumenical activities. Although in its organizational structure it is not officially a part of either the National Council or the World Council of Churches, in practice it represents and serves them both. In its own character, it reflects the concern for the church in its more than denominational dimension, which is of the genius of the ecumenical movement. It is a visible reminder that there is a unity in Christ wider than that experienced in one's own parish. Unfortunately, it sometimes happens that a minister who has been attracted by the dramatic aspects of world-wide ecumenical assemblies is less ecumenical when it means continuous and prosaic relationships with Christians of other historic backgrounds in his own community. He may even merit the cynical remark that his ecumenical enthusiasm is in inverse ratio to his distance from home. If so, he needs to be reminded of Gilbert Keith Chesterton's epigram that nothing is real unless it is local. For most

Christians, their best opportunity of being ecumenical is through full and loyal participation in the Council of Churches that is nearest to them.

ECUMENICAL AND DENOMINATIONAL

Whether a local church will be effectively ecumenical will usually depend on the viewpoint of its minister. A special responsibility therefore rests on the theological seminaries which provide the ministerial leadership for each denomination. Many of the seminaries are seeking to find their true role in ecumenical education, but others are only touching the surface of the problem. It is certainly not solved by giving a course in the history of the ecumenical movement. That is only adding one more subject to an already overloaded curriculum. It is hardly solved by establishing a chair of ecumenics. That is treating ecumenical interests too much like a department of the church's concern. It is not solved by training some promising men for posts in ecumenical organizations. That tends to imply that ecumenical work is the task of a special few. Ecumenical education is a dimension of the entire life of the church—its worship, its preaching, its teaching, its theology, its conception of the ministry, its understanding of its history, its relation to society, and its role in the community and the world. To get an ecumenical viewpoint in this sense in the theological school and in local churches for which it provides the ministry is what is required if the false antithesis between ecumenical and local is to be resolved.

Whether the local church will really regard itself as an embodiment of the Church Ecumenical will also be greatly affected by the attitude of the leaders of the denomination to which it belongs. Candor compels the admission that although the denominations as national bodies are officially committed to co-operation with one another, many of them do not take a strong initiative in establishing co-operation as a determinative policy for the local church. When the Methodist district superintendent or the Presbyterian synodical executive begins to ask the local churches of their areas not only how many new members were received and how much was contributed to benevolences but how much interchurch co-operation they practiced, and in what ways, we may expect to see far greater ecumenical progress.

At the present stage in the ecumenical movement, the churches do most things, and the most important things, separately, and do only a few things together. The acid test of the denominations' commitment to the Church Ecumenical is whether they are glad to see the balance reversed, and to keep moving on to a day when they will be doing most things together, and only a few things separately.

Consider what our denominations might do together now—quite within the present system—if the ecumenical spirit were to express itself fully in ecumenical action. We might, for example, pool our resources for missionary expansion on a far more extensive scale and within a common strategy. We might arrive at firm comity agreements under which we would establish all new churches by a co-operative process for best serving the Kingdom of God even if it did not enhance denominational prestige. In every important area of responsibility, we might develop interdenominational policies based on the kind of thorough research which is gravely lacking today because it is too expensive for a denomination to pursue alone.

An unhappy illustration of how far we still have to go before denominational practice measures up to denominational profession is afforded by a recent development in one of the Caribbean islands. In a conference of leaders of the several denominations, it was unanimously agreed that over-all strategy for the years ahead required a full-time executive for the Council of Churches in the island. This was no casual decision. In an interdenominational consultation, it had been clearly envisaged as the number one priority for evangelical advance in a situation where former comity arrangements were breaking down as a result of rapid population changes. For the new common responsibility, two pastors were nominated as best qualified. But when the national agencies of their respective denominations were approached, the reaction of each was that it "could not spare" the man in question. It is hard to escape the conclusion that each was placing an immediate denominational interest above the long-range interest of the Christian community as a whole.

An unexpected by-product of the ecumenical advance of the last generation appears to be a heightening of denominational and confessional self-consciousness. This may be either good or bad in its consequences—bad if it results in a defensive posture, in less readiness to hear the word that God is speaking through other churches, or in an absorption in promoting a denomination's own institutional interests; good if it stimulates a denomination to examine its own historical tradition and to gain a surer understanding of its distinctive contribution to ecumenical Christianity. In the words of William Temple at his enthronement as Archbishop of Canterbury in 1942: "We shall impoverish our service of the wider fellowship if we let our membership of our own Communion become hesitant or indefinite."[5]

The denominational self-consciousness is especially evident in the new vigor of the world-wide confessional bodies, such as the Lambeth Conference of the Anglican Communion, the Lutheran World Federation, the World Presbyterian Alliance, the Baptist World Alliance, and the World Methodist Council.[6] In principle, they are not in conflict with the ecumenical movement. On the contrary, they may strengthen it in an important way—by educating their own special constituencies to understand and support the ecumenical movement. Millions of Christians who will never be directly reached by the World Council of Churches could be given an ecumenical orientation through the confessional bodies. These bodies would at the same time

[5] *The Church Looks Forward* (London: The Macmillan Company, 1944), p. 4.
[6] Other bodies of similar type are the International Congregational Council, the World Convention of Churches of Christ (Disciples), the Friends' World Committee, the Mennonite World Conference, and the Pentecostal World Conference. Two world-wide confessional bodies—Lutheran and Presbyterian—have established their headquarters in Geneva in order to facilitate effective co-operation with the World Council of Churches.

be demonstrating that the ecumenical movement does not involve the reduction of diverse historical traditions to a residuum of faith, but rather provides a rich synthesis. Viewed in this light, all of the confessional bodies can be helpfully ecumenical. Any of them, however, could easily become counter-ecumenical. It would do so if its activities were such as to encourage local churches to feel self-sufficient in their denominationalism and satisfied with a fragmented church.

Chapter VIII

THE FAR HORIZON OF THE ROAD

The Goal of the Ecumenical Movement

Up to this point, we have considered the ecumenical movement in terms of the increasing unity that is possible within a system of co-operating denominations. We now raise the question whether the ultimate goal of our hopes is that the denominations should be superseded by a united structure in a single body. This is the great unsettled issue in the ecumenical movement of today.

Among thoughtful students of the problem, union is not advocated for the sake of bigness. Although there are certain values in size, there is considerable historical evidence that great bodies tend to be less creative than those that are smaller and more closely knit. Nor is union sought just for the sake of practical efficiency. Although there is indubitable inefficiency in the constant duplication of denominational activities, the standardized pattern of a chain-store organization is no model for the spiritual realm.

Such arguments as those based on size and efficiency never get to the heart of the matter. The basic consideration lies at a far deeper level. It is whether union has any inherent connection with the mission of the church in the world. That mission is most plainly indicated in our Lord's word, "And I, when I am lifted up from the earth, will draw all men to myself" (John 12:32). The church exists to draw men to Christ—not to some dynamic leader, not to a doctrinal system, not to a form of government, not to a special interpretation of Scripture or sacraments. Whenever a church points to any of these things in a way that obscures its sole mission of drawing men to Christ, it stands in need of correction.

WHY UNITY MATTERS

The great weakness of a denomination is that it does exactly this. It does not mean to do so. It may not realize that it is doing so. Yet it is for such secondary reasons that the denomination, as such, comes into being. That is why a great Presbyterian missionary leader, Robert E. Speer, once said that he was glad the adjective "Presbyterian" could not be effectively translated into Chinese. Each denomination, in its separate existence as a denomination, testifies to the insight of some vigorous founder, to a form of polity, to a mode of worship, to a certain view of baptism or the Eucharist, to the effect of cultural differences, or to some special historical circumstance. Each of these testimonies may have its own value, but not as the ground of existence of a Christian Church.

The only ground for existence as church is to draw men to Christ. Anything which makes that less luminous is open to challenge. That is why St. Paul so sharply criticized what he saw happening among Christians in Corinth. They were drawing attention to figures like Paul and Peter and Apollos (I Cor. 1:10–17) and thereby dimming the truth that there is "no other foundation" than Jesus Christ.

All denominations are, of course, in their various ways, testifying to Christ. But their separate traditions make this witness less concentrated and distinct, and their insistence on a continuing separateness beclouds the sole reason for His Church. Each denomination is unconsciously saying to the world that it regards something else than Christ as justifying it in remaining apart from others who have the same loyalty to Him. In some cases, this means that even in the most sacred act of corporate communion with the Head of the Church, attention is drawn to an excluding definition of His Table.

The tragic seriousness of our separations is most obvious in lands in which non-Christians are in the great majority and a little Christian community has a hard struggle to bear any visible testimony at all. In such an environment, it is self-defeating to point to anything other than its fundamental reason for being. That is why the most urgent appeals for union have come from the churches of Asia. They have long been saying to the churches of the West, "To you, union may seem optional, but among us it is indispensable to our witness to Christ." Their situation is reminiscent of that which the earliest church confronted. Peter and Paul might have very serious differences—as, for example, in the matter of circumcision and the significance of the Jewish law (Acts 15 and Gal. 2), but they knew that they must hold their differences in a way that would not split the Christian community and thereby blur its witness to Christ in a non-Christian world.

A visible unity of the church appears still more urgent when we reflect on the significance of its gospel for society at large. The church is trying to tell the world that the reconciliation of its clashing peoples and divided communities can be achieved through Christ. But the world will surely be skeptical until the church which makes the claim gives clearer evidence of that reconciling power in its own institutional life. The most devastating comment on the present denominational system is that its existence is a tacit admission that the church is itself infected with the same kind of factionalism which its gospel is supposed to overcome. The church thus looks like only another ordinary association, based on men's opinions and preferences, rather than the beginning of a New Creation in Christ. If we are to persuade the world that Christ, whose Body the church is, can really reconcile divided nations and races and classes, we will have to give a much more convincing demonstration that the churches know the meaning of reconciliation in their own relation to one another.

INNER SPIRIT AND OUTER FORM

At this point, the rejoinder is sure to be made that real unity is a matter of inner spirit, not of outer form, and that the question of organization is therefore of no importance. That the spirit is fundamental we must indeed agree. But in the Christian view, spirit and body are not separable. To make a sharp division between the two is to contradict the nature of Christianity. For at the center of all biblical faith is a doctrine of creation which affirms that the visible world is an expression of the Spirit of God, and at the center of the Christian gospel is a doctrine of incarnation which declares that He has been made manifest in the flesh. This must put us on guard against any assumption that it can ever be inconsequential whether the spirit finds embodiment or not. In the frequently quoted statement of William Temple, Christianity is "the most materialistic of the world's great religions." In it, body and spirit are not antithetical but correlative parts of a vital whole. In proportion as spirit is genuine and strong, it clothes itself in an appropriate outward form.

If, to take a familiar example from daily life, there is a true spirit of unity between husband and wife and children, it does not remain hidden. It is objectified in the social institution of the family as the material framework that provides for mutual interests. This is both the visible manifestation of the invisible spirit and the means of continually reinforcing it. We would not think of excusing neglect of a carefully planned pattern of family life on the plea that "spiritual unity" is the only thing that counts.

That the unity of the church, like that of a family, is ultimately a quality of spirit is completely true. If unity does not involve, first and always, the kind of Christian love described in I Corinthians 13, it is not worth the attention we are giving to it. Far more poignant than any scandal of splitting into different denominations is the scandal of falling so far short of our Lord's standard that "by this all men will know that you are my disciples, if you have love for one another" (John 13:35).

Although the seventeenth chapter of the Gospel according to John is often cited in advocacy of church union, a careful exegesis makes it clear that what our Lord is here emphasizing is the underlying unity of spirit. The prayer "that they may all be one" is followed by the explicit definition, "as Thou, Father, art in me and I in Thee," which can only refer to a unity of personal relationships. But the passage lends no support to the contention that a unity that is "spiritual" in the sense of being unembodied is the only thing that matters. Our Lord's prayer for the oneness of His followers adds plainly that this is in order "that the world may believe." It follows from this that the unity must be of such a nature as can be recognized and understood by those outside the Christian fellowship. A unity that is unseen by the world can never persuade the world to believe.

When we ask how the oneness in spirit is to be given a body which will be both fully recognizable and effective, we confront a problem so complex as to raise the question whether agreement can ever be within the range of practical churchmanship. As things now stand, many earnest Christians are definitely opposed to anything like organizational union on a large scale. It is important to discern clearly why this is so.

WHY UNION IS FEARED

Among those opposed to union, we should distinguish between two very different groups. One consists of those too limited in historical understanding and ecumenical contacts to move out into any realm of thought beyond the denominational tradition to which they are accustomed. Christians of this type need most of all to be exposed to a wider vision and experience. There are other critics, however, who are sensitive to the evils of denominationalism. They are really concerned for the wholeness of the church. They are committed to a co-operative fellowship. But they stop decisively short of union. They even fear it. They suspect that it would mean a sacrifice of precious values of the past. Especially they fear that in any great ecclesiastical structure hard-won freedoms would be lost, and overcentralized and bureaucratic practices strengthened.

For those who are distrustful of union for this reason, we should have full respect. The course of church history through the centuries lends no little justification to their misgiving. We shall be wise to listen to them sympathetically. Unless we can all be assured that union would not result in the loss of rightful liberty and of rich diversity, we may well settle for growing co-operation rather than urge "one great church."

The informed resistance to union rests largely on a general distrust of institutionalism. It knows that when any organization becomes strong enough to monopolize a field, it faces a subtle temptation to exercise conformist pressures and controls as a means of furthering its own interests. The largest of all the Christian communions has given an historical illustration of the kind of authoritarian and regimented structure that we do not want. And it is a monolithic institution of some such type which many Protestants conjure up in their imaginations as soon as they hear of any proposal for church union. Let us say, so forthrightly that we cannot be misunderstood, that this is not the kind of unity we seek.

To escape the ecclesiastical anarchy of a host of competing denominations, however, does not require leaping into an ecclesiastical imperialism. The issue is how to secure the kind of unity in diversity which is described in I Corinthians 12. In order to think clearly and carefully about the problem, we must distinguish among four different meanings that the phrase, "the unity of the church," now has in the minds of various people.[1]

First, there is the unity of *spiritual fellowship*. For those who place the entire emphasis here, the problem of structure is negli-

[1] In this outline of alternative views, I follow, in the main, the same classification as Henry P. Van Dusen's in "The Significance of Conciliar Ecumenicity," *Ecumenical Review*, April, 1960 (Vol. XII, No. 3), pp. 314-315, although in a different order and emphasis.

gible. Mutual appreciation and good will based on the recognition of a common relation to Christ represent all the unity that they deem necessary.

Second, going further than inner attitude, is the unity of *co-operative association and action*. This is the kind of unity now found in Councils of Churches—local, national, and world-wide. It rests on the federative principle increasingly adopted in the last fifty years.

Third, going beyond both inner attitude and organization for working together in various tasks, is the unity of *mutual recognition*. This would involve, when fully achieved, interdenominational understandings and agreements which would provide not only a freely transferable membership but also a ministry accepted by all the sacraments open to all. This is often labeled intercommunion.

Fourth, there is the conception of unity which rejects the denominational system, even if characterized by a co-operative spirit and a mutual recognition of ministries and sacraments, and seeks to bring all Christians into *a single church* with a common doctrinal basis and a common administrative structure.

It is usually assumed that union of this last type, commonly called "organic," necessarily involves much centralized control. This seems to me to be a serious misconception. A body is an organism if it consists of mutually connected and mutually dependent parts, so constituted as to function as a living whole. A unity is therefore rightly described as organic if a single stream of life flows through all the parts and if no part is shut off from any aspect of the common experience. Thus conceived, organic unity as applied to the church need not involve a centralized control. It would, however, mean at least three things which are not true of the churches today. These three are: (1) an interchangeable membership, so that a Christian who belongs to any congregation may be received as a member by any other congregation; (2) a ministry which is everywhere accepted as the ministry of the entire church; (3) sacraments of universal validity to which all church members are welcome.

Granted these three essentials of an organic life, the question of how the church should be organized and governed is a separate matter, one which may be decided in the light of experience and practical advantages and disadvantages. There might be a substantial measure of central direction or there might be a bare minimum. In either case, the unity of the church would be organic if it assured to each Christian full participation in the life of the whole.

That organic unity in this sense is possible without legal or coercive control from the center is shown by the fact that Christians who now live under a congregational polity actually have an experience of such unity. When there is a common tradition expressed in characteristic ways, when there is a common ministry of the Word and sacraments, when there is a common Christian commitment and a common program of service, when there is a strong sense of Christian fellowship, the members of a loosely knit structure may be unmistakably one body and have a recognizable identity which remains true to type generation after generation. If this is true now within a denomination, it could become similarly true in a wider union.

We ought not, therefore, to assume that in order to be truly organic the church must have a highly centralized administration. The heart of organic unity is not a particular type of organization but a fully shared experience in a fully interconnected life.

CORPORATE UNION VS. FEDERATION WITH INTERCOMMUNION

Whether we call it "organic" or not, we can envisage a kind of unity which goes beyond co-operation in common tasks and yet does not go so far as to merge all denominations into one administrative structure. The possible alternative is a strong federation combined with full intercommunion. This would, however, require radical changes in the conception of a denomination's authority. It would call for firm agreements between the denominations which would limit their independence to the extent of assuring to the Christian community as a whole a common membership, a common ministry, common sacraments, and a common organ of co-ordinated action. If these goals were all achieved, the result would be a markedly different ecclesiastical climate from that in which we now live, even though denominations still remained as different types of organization within the Christian community, each possessing administrative functions within defined limits.

Beyond close federation and full intercommunion, however, there is the vision, cherished by prophetic spirits in all of the historic traditions, of a union in which denominations gladly give up their separate existences and come together in a new structural pattern. This is most accurately designated as "corporate" union—corporate in the exact and literal sense that when the process is complete there is one body, with an administration that embraces all. Is this the final goal we seek through the ecumenical movement?

Between this type of corporate union and strong federation with intercommunion, the choice must eventually be made. The ecumenical developments of our time have already gone too far to permit us to be satisfied with an inherited system in which denominations regard themselves as wholly sovereign—even to the point of rejecting one another's ministries, excluding one another from sacramental worship, and launching new parishes in a way that clearly weakens the churches of other Christians. The question now is whether anything short of corporate union can be a sufficient manifestation of the church as a single Reality given to us by Jesus Christ in and with the gospel.

If we are thinking in world-wide terms, it is difficult to believe that corporate union is the answer in any foreseeable future. The world is too big and too complex for a single government. The extreme differences in language and culture and in social and political circumstance make a universal administration almost out of the question. The Roman Catholic Church, it is true, has a considerable measure of world government, but it is secured at the unfortunate price of submissive and uncritical acceptance of an earthly authority from which there is no appeal.

The critics of the ecumenical movement who assume that it is committed to some such superchurch on a world-wide scale are looking at a figment of their own imagination. There is not one confessional group in the entire ecumenical household that accepts a pattern of a single, international administration for itself —to say nothing of accepting it for the church collectively. Even the Eastern Orthodox, with all their emphasis on being the one Holy Catholic Church, do not have an administrative organization of world-wide scope. Their various national or regional units are administratively independent—autocephalous, to use their term—held together only by the force of a common tradition of faith and worship. In the world-wide Anglican communion, which greatly cherishes its Catholic heritage, there is no central organ of control or government. It secures a regional decentralization in administration by assuring autonomy to the church in each country. The Lambeth Conference of all the bishops has great influence, but is a wholly advisory body. The international structures of other communions—such as the Lutheran World Federation, the World Presbyterian Alliance, and the Methodist World Council—likewise have no regulatory powers. If even a confessional family in which there are only minor divergencies in order and government does not find it practicable to have a universal authority, it is farfetched indeed to suppose that an ecumenical church, drawing many diverse families together, would or could do so.

On the international level, then, it is the processes of conference and co-operation, not of ecclesiastical legislation, on which we must rely to achieve our unity. The Christian world community is best conceived in terms not of administrative authority or control imposed from the center but of a closely knit fellowship of national or regional bodies, all of which are in full communion with one another, have a ministry and sacraments common to all, and possess an effective instrument for continuous consultation on policy and strategy, for common planning in the whole range of program, and for such limited operational responsibilities as may be committed to it. A strengthened World Council of Churches could be the organ of this world community.

UNITY AT NATIONAL LEVELS

Within national or regional areas, however, it is reasonable to seek corporate union as a final goal. Although the problems involved are more complex and baffling than is usually realized, there is nothing except our own restricted vision to make union at the national level impracticable. Each of the larger denominations has already demonstrated the workability of a great church with millions of members—and members of very different theological convictions. Indeed, within a single denomination, one can see today virtually the whole range of viewpoints to be found among denominations. Yet these divergent members hold together in one body. Moreover, there has already been sufficient successful experiment in corporate union, in America and elsewhere, to encourage bold advance. Within the span of the half century reviewed in this volume, there have been at least forty unions in different parts of the world. Ten of them have involved churches of different confessional backgrounds or of different forms of polity.[2]

The Church of South India is a noteworthy demonstration that it is possible to bridge even the gulf between churches that insist on the historic episcopacy and those whose traditions have had no place for it. In North India and Pakistan and Ceylon, proposals for union even more inclusive than in South India are now at the point of decision. If they are consummated, we may see a church which spans the separations not only in the ministry and the Lord's Supper but in baptism as well.

Whether there will be any general progress on the road to union by churches of the ecumenical movement seems to me to depend chiefly on one condition. That condition is whether there is a readiness to provide for a very large measure of freedom and

[2] Included in the unions that crossed major denominational lines are the Church of South India, the North India United Church, the United Church of Canada, the Church of Christ in Japan, the Church of Christ in China, the United Church of Christ in the Philippine Islands, the Church of Christ in Thailand, the Church of Central Africa, the United Evangelical Church of Puerto Rico, and the United Church of Christ now in process of formation in the United States.

diversity within the united church. The great roadblock is the lurking fear that union would result in standardization and regimentation.

That fear is not to be casually dismissed. Union really could result in too much conformism to a single pattern of thought, too little flexibility for experiment, too easy squelching of minorities. It might mean too much of the kind of unity achieved by the drill sergeant who makes everyone "toe the line." The fear of this must be offset by convincing evidence that the union we are seeking is one which makes room for a wide range of differences.

The misgiving about the regimentation that might go with "one great church" leads many thoughtful Christians to prefer federation to union. Their position calls for careful scrutiny. If it means the perpetuation of the more than two hundred and fifty organizations now listed in the *Yearbook of American Churches*, we must view the prospect with a sinking heart. The process of fragmentation long ago reached the point of absurdity. Many of the denominations owe their autonomous existence to cultural, sociological, economic, and political influences that have little or nothing to do with doctrine or worship or principle of order. They therefore have no Christian ground for permanent separation.

There are, however, a few types of churches—you could count them on your fingers—that represent important differences of Christian conviction. If the present miscellany of denominations were gradually reduced by a series of mergers to these few types, a good case could be made for their continuance in a closely federated structure—always provided they could come to basic agreements for a ministry recognized by all and a Lord's Table at which all could meet. If these barriers remain, federation inevitably falls short of the Christian requirement. "Something there is that doesn't love a wall,"[3] and this should prove most true of those who are most conscious of their unity in Christ.

Those who favor federation feel that different types of Chris-

---

[3] Robert Frost, "Mending Wall," *North of Boston* (New York: Henry Holt and Company, 1914), p. 11.

tians ought not to be expected to live in the same ecclesiastical dwelling. Their viewpoint is pictured well in a figure of speech once used by a Russian Orthodox scholar. He suggested that association in the Christian community should be like that in an old-fashioned Russian household living in quarters divided into several compartments which permit the different members to feel at home with their own style of arrangements but which have doors opening so freely that none is excluded from a common family life.

It is the unwillingness to tolerate differences which has been the most prolific source of division throughout Christian history. If we are to move beyond federation to corporate union on a large scale, a fundamental psychological requirement is the recognition of the validity of substantial differences within the united church.

DIFFERENCES IN A UNITED CHURCH

The assumption that each major difference in doctrine or worship or polity justifies existence as an independent denomination overlooks the crucial point that when a difference is maintained in isolation it gets out of proper balance. If differences are complementary, they belong together. Otherwise, as William Temple said, "it is as though in one man's veins there were only red corpuscles and in another only white." "The total of both," he went on, "might be the right supply for both men, but health depends on their being mixed." And he commented that "every part of the Church now suffers more or less from one-sided development; the true balance is found nowhere."[4] As another wise British Christian, J. H. Oldham, says, "Differences were meant by God not to divide but to enrich."[5] This truth is directly contrary to the idea that only those who think alike and worship alike belong in the same church.

[4] *Personal Religion and the Life of Fellowship* (London: Longmans, Green and Company, 1926), p. 30.
[5] H. N. Bate (ed.), *Faith and Order: Lausanne, 1927* (London: SCM Press, 1927), p. 359.

In early centuries, the conception of unity as a uniformity that could not tolerate differences meant the exclusion of dissenters by ecclesiastical authority. In later centuries, political coercion was added to the ecclesiastical. Both of these methods failed long before the Reformation, as is shown by the emergence of sects like the Donatists and the Monophysites and by the great split between the Greek Church of the East and the Latin Church of the West. After the Reformation, the main bodies of Protestantism still conceived unity as uniformity, with even more fissiparous results. In America, when the civil power was no longer invoked to support the ecclesiastical, the prospect of unity was almost abandoned, except for a few prophetic voices and a few sporadic projects, until the present century. All these developments underscore the mistake of identifying unity with uniformity.

This aspect of institutional history is well summarized by Winfred E. Garrison as a movement in three stages from "unity by exclusion" to "unity by compulsion," and finally to the "eclipse of the unity ideal."[6] He concludes that the only kind of united church which is either attainable or desirable is one which grants "complete liberty" within itself for *every* viewpoint as to doctrine or order or practice that any group may interpret as Christian. This is too extreme a conclusion. His "united church" would be an amorphous collection of miscellaneous groups, not a corporate community in any recognizable sense. It would not have enough of a body of common conviction to mark it off as distinctive or to prevent it from being swallowed up by the world. It would not ensure the maintenance of a continuing identity from generation to generation. What Garrison unconsciously does is to reduce the meaning of a united church to little more than friendly good will among all who desire to call themselves Christians. A general Christian atmosphere is thus substituted for a united church.

This brings us face to face with the question, how much agreement in doctrine, how much of a common pattern of worship,

[6] *Quest and Character of a United Church* (Nashville: Abingdon Press, 1957).

how much of a co-ordination of activities through some organized oversight, are essential for corporate union and a united church?

As for doctrine, the first requirement is to recognize how much of a real consensus, even though not explicitly formulated, there actually is among the churches of the ecumenical movement. On the basis of their understanding of the Bible, they share a common faith in God and His forgiving love, in Christ and His redeeming power, in the Holy Spirit and His renewing work in the Christian community. Here is a solid substratum of Christian doctrine about which there is nothing denominational; it is the common tradition of the great central stream of Christianity. Perhaps this heart of the historic Christian faith really furnishes enough doctrinal foundation for the beginning of a united church. Within that church, different groups would, of course, contend for different interpretations. Within it, various groups would hold additional doctrines while standing together on a firm common ground. When one reflects on the theological divergences even among Paul, Peter, John, and the author of the Epistle to the Hebrews, as mirrored in the New Testament, he must conclude that it is not necessary for all Christians to hold an identical theological system.

The relation of doctrine to unity is often misconceived. Profound convictions are certainly essential to any vertebrate Christian community. But the difference between faith and any particular propositions in which the faith is expressed and communicated must always be borne in mind. No intellectual formulation is ever the real basis of unity in the church. Unity lies at a much deeper level. It lies in the experience of finding that God meets us in Christ and in our response to Him in faith. This experience impels us to seek agreement in our verbal expression of it, but we must not identify the faith with the formula. To do so is to over-intellectualize the nature of the Christian gospel.

The definition of the faith is the work of the Christian community. The development of a fully articulated theology, accordingly, is a function of the united church rather than a precondition of it. The community of faith and love comes first, and agreement in doctrinal statements grows out of this—not vice versa.[7]

Within the united church there will, of course, be endless theological debate in the process of defining, refining, elaborating, and systematizing the doctrine, but this will be a sign of healthy vigor provided it takes place within an ecumenical fellowship and moves in the orbit of the central proclamation that "God was in Christ reconciling the world unto Himself." The progress of the ecumenical movement during our lifetime strongly suggests that the path of advance toward a united church is that of always treating the Christian fellowship as primary, and expecting that as this becomes more of an experienced reality, doctrinal consensus will likewise increase.

This judgment is reinforced by reflecting on the record in the Gospels. Our Lord did not begin by setting up a complete system of doctrine and then asking those who accepted it to follow Him. He invited them to accept Himself and on this basis to become associated with Him. The community of Christ's people was the prius. The development of doctrine took place within the community gathered around Him.

As for forms of worship, it is already clear that they do not constitute an insurmountable barrier to unity. That different types of worship are both valid and valuable is now generally agreed. The silence of the Quaker meeting, the informal warmth of the "free church" congregation, and the reverent dignity of the liturgical service may all have an appropriate place in a united church.

At the point of sacramental worship, however, there are grave difficulties, especially in the case of the Lord's Supper. This involves the vexing problem of intercommunion, and it seems probable that the present barrier can be removed only as the problem of a common ministry is solved—a subject to which we give extended attention a little later.

[7] For an exceedingly helpful exposition of this view see Albert C. Outler, *The Christian Tradition and the Unity We Seek* (New York: Oxford University Press, 1957).

In the case of baptism, a solution of the existing impasse may be found through an arrangement flexible enough to permit optional practices. Although the meaning and the form of baptism are still debatable issues, the conflicting views do not follow denominational lines as sharply as hitherto. Within the Presbyterian and Reformed family, for example, Karl Barth is a conspicuous spokesman for the position that baptism only of adults who have made their own decision is preferable. He sees this as essential to maintaining a clearer distinction between the church and the world. Within denominations like the Baptist and the Disciples of Christ, on the other hand, which have historically stood for believer's baptism by immersion, the values of a dedicatory service marking the incorporation of the child into the Christian household are now more widely appreciated.

The Problem of a Common Order

Of all the issues that make union on any comprehensive scale appear utopian, the most stubborn lie in the field of ecclesiastical order. At first thought, these might seem to be relatively easy of solution. Why should they not be dealt with on the basis of practical experience and an objective weighing of the advantages and disadvantages of different forms of church government? The difficulty is that for a large part of the Christian community—those who put the heaviest accent on the Catholic heritage—the question is one not merely of pragmatic values but of faith. For them, it involves not only matters of organization, but the basic issue whether there is one—and only one—divine plan for the order of the church as the Body of Christ in the world.

More specifically, the Catholic—whether of the Roman, the Greek, or of the Anglican type—insists that it is integral to God's pattern for the church that it have bishops in an apostolic succession, that a full and valid ministry depends upon ordination by such bishops, and that the Eucharist is properly administered only by those thus ordained. Is it possible for the gulf between the Catholic and the general Protestant viewpoints to be bridged?

It is popularly assumed that Protestants are wholly uninterested in any kind of apostolic succession. This, however, is a misconception. Together with all other Christians, they cherish the Christian community as continuous with the first community that gathered around our Lord and His apostles. As an actual fact of history, there is such a continuity that has never been broken. It is a succession of the *church as a whole*, not merely of its ministers. It is the church rather than any group within it which is most truly apostolic, just as it was the whole Christian community, not apostles or bishops or ministers, to whom the Spirit was given at Pentecost. The essential succession is the priesthood of believers, going back in a straight line to Christ. To carry on this succession is the prerogative of every faithful member of the Christian community.

It is important, therefore, to emphasize the distinction between this "apostolic succession" and the historic episcopate. The episcopate has an honored and venerable place in the Christian community, but it is the church that makes the episcopacy, not the episcopacy that makes the church. The Catholic can adduce no historical verification of an unbroken line of ordination by bishops in actual succession with the apostles. There is, however, a general consensus of scholarly opinion that by the middle of the second century the church had developed an episcopally ordained ministry which was regarded as possessing an authority connected with that given by the Lord to the apostles.[8] This tradition was one of the important ways of safeguarding the apostolic teaching from corruption in any part of the world.

The question, of course, is rightly raised whether the apostles could really have "successors" in any accurate sense of the word. The church is built upon "the foundation of the apostles" (Eph. 2:20) but, as has been acutely observed, a foundation does not repeat itself. The apostolate was unique and nontransmissible, thus not permitting us to think of the episcopate as its official prolongation. Moreover, most objective students of the subject hold with Bishop J. B. Lightfoot that historical evidence indi-

[8] See, e.g., Hans Lietzmann, *The Founding of the Church Universal*, trans. Bertram L. Woolf (New York: Charles Scribner's Sons, 1938), pp. 73-87.

cates that the episcopate as a general office covering a diocesan area "was formed not out of the apostolic order by localization but out of the presbyteral by elevation."[9]

However much they may differ about the historical origins and the theory of the episcopate, most Christians can see in it an efficacious symbol of the continuity and unity of the church. Although there is no biblical evidence for regarding episcopacy as necessary, there is good reason to conclude that it was a normal development. Despite the fact that there is no ground for assuming that God has bound Himself to grant greater blessing or grace through the bishop than through other ministers, the oversight of the church through carefully chosen representative personalities can be and has been valuable. This is altogether different from saying that where there is no bishop there is no true church.

From the standpoint of human probability, it seems clear that if there is ever to be a ministry recognized throughout the whole church, it will be one in which the historic episcopate plays an important role. The great majority of the Christians of the world have the episcopate today. It would be presumptuous to expect them to give it up in deference to a minority. And on the intrinsic merits of the case, why should not Christians generally be prepared to include bishops in the structure of their church—provided, first, that this does not involve any controversial interpretation of the nature of episcopacy, and, second, that it is surrounded with constitutional safeguards against its being exercised in an arbitrary manner? Some form of oversight is required in every ecclesiastical polity, although it may be designated "superintendent" or "secretary" rather than "bishop." Even among the strong champions of the autonomy of the local church, the importance of effective means of cohesion is increasingly recognized.

If episcopacy is interpreted as necessary to the existence of the church and its ministry, there is no prospect of its being universally accepted. To make such an interpretation a *sine qua non* of union is to make union out of the question. Why should a united

---

[9] J. B. Lightfoot, "The Christian Ministry," *St. Paul's Epistle to the Philippians* (4th ed., London, 1879), p. 196.

church be expected to have an interpretation which is not required even within a single communion, like the Anglican, which
greatly treasures the episcopacy?

Within the Anglican communion today, there are three different theological views about the episcopate. One holds it to be of
the *"esse"* of the Church. Another says "No," that it is of the
"bene esse." A third position regards it as of the *"plene esse."* If
all these interpretations coexist even within Anglicanism, why not
within a greater church? Why can we not unite in accepting
episcopacy as a natural historical development in the Christian
community, and then discuss its theology as much as desired for
generations to come? This is what is contemplated in the current
plans for union in North India, Pakistan, and Ceylon. The Cey-
lonese proposal puts it in this way:

> The uniting Churches accept the historic episcopate in a constitu-
> tional form. . . . By historic episcopate is meant the episcopate which
> has historic continuity with the undivided Church. No particular theo-
> logical interpretation of episcopacy shall be demanded.[10]

If churches that do not now have the episcopate were to adopt
it, without adopting any special theory of it, as an appropriate
instrument of order in a united church, how could the existing
ministries of the uniting denominations be so combined as to
establish a ministry universally recognized? Obviously, non-
Anglicans could not be expected to undergo a reordination which
would be a tacit admission that their past ministry had been un-
apostolic or invalid. On the other hand, there would seem to be
no serious reason why there might not be a mutual extension of
the several ministries. Why might not all of the clergy receive a
new commission which would qualify each of them to minister
to Christians coming into the united church from other bodies
than his own?

This is the method of unification of ministries now under consideration in North India, Pakistan, and Ceylon. It is proposed

[10] *Negotiating Committee, Scheme of Church Union in Ceylon, Madras,
and Colombo* (United Society for Christian Literature, 1949), pp. 18–19.

that at the inception of the united church, all ministers would participate in a great service in which each would receive, from both bishops and other representatives of the uniting churches, a commission and authority for a wider ministry in the church as a whole.[11]

By such a unification of the ministries, the problem of ensuring a celebration of the Eucharist acceptable to all would also be solved. It would in one stroke cut the Gordian knot that has perpetuated the sad spectacle of division in what ought to be the great feast of Christian unity.

The ecumenical movement is not committed to this or any other project for effecting a united structure of the church. It is, however, giving increasing study to the nature of the unity that Christians should be striving toward. Coming before the 1961 Assembly of the World Council of Churches is a statement drafted by its Commission on Faith and Order as a preliminary attempt to define some of the essential lineaments of a united church. In a single, closely packed sentence, it is characterized as one

which brings all in each place who confess Christ Jesus as Lord into a fully committed fellowship with one another through one baptism into Him, holding the one apostolic faith, preaching the one gospel and breaking the one bread, and having a corporate life reaching out in witness and service to all; and which at the same time unites them with the whole Christian fellowship in all places and all ages in such wise that ministry and members are acknowledged by all, and that all can act and speak together as occasion requires for the tasks to which God calls the Church.[12]

The more this concise statement is studied, the more it commends itself as a true signpost indicating the kind of goal we seek,

[11] This is also a main feature of the plan proposed by Eugene Carson Blake and Bishop James A. Pike on December 4, 1960, for the union of the United Presbyterian Church in the U.S.A., the Protestant Episcopal Church, the Methodist Church, and the United Church of Christ. See the *Christian Century*, December 21, 1960.
[12] The full report is published in the *Ecumenical Review*, October, 1960 (Vol. XIII: No. 1).

though without suggesting means of reaching the goal. One of the noteworthy aspects is the insistence that all the Christians in a local community or neighborhood belong together in one visible fellowship. They are not to hive off into separate societies determined by personal preferences and the congeniality of a group. They worship and work together because they have the same mission to fulfill as the one People of God in that place.

How much central administration would be desirable in a united church is a question to be answered in the light of experience rather than by a priori considerations. Each of the three historical types of polity—episcopal, presbyterian, congregational—has embodied important values. Each has also its limitations; there is no perfect system of government. The crux of the problem is always to find the right balance between order and freedom. The polity of a united church must take up and blend together the proved values of each historic type and avoid the danger of imbalance in either direction.

In general, the danger of too much central authority is greater than that of too little. Any significant unity within a body that includes wide diversities must depend on voluntary response to effective leadership far more than on prescribed regulations. A united church that operated on any other assumption would not remain united. There is no reason, however, why a united church might not ensure as large a degree of decentralization as it found desirable by providing for regional administrations with relatively little direction from "the top."

GROUNDS FOR HOPE

The experience of the last fifty years justifies the hope that a united Church in America, including most of the denominations which now constitute the National Council, and some others as well, is really possible. If, a half century ago, anyone had been bold enough to predict that within the lifetime of living men there would be an ecumenical movement such as we see today, he would have been called a visionary. Yet here it is, burgeoning with vigorous life, and, in the sober judgment of a historian like

Kenneth S. Latourette, affording promise of being as significant for the future as was the Reformation of the sixteenth century.[13] In the light of what has happened in the last fifty years, we need not expect the next fifty years to be limited to what we can now forecast. There is no reason why the churches, if they keep moving steadily forward, may not reach a goal that lies far beyond our present ken.

The emergence of the World Council means that at last there is a Christian community within which the churches mutually recognize each other as churches. Some of them may regard others as deficient in certain respects, but their continuing participation in the Council testifies to the actual existence of a unity at a deeper level than any or all of their differences. As the implications of this unprecedented development become more clearly perceived and as the imagination of Christian people generally glimpses the vision of new possibilities, who can set limits to what they may hear the Holy Spirit saying to the churches?

A primary condition of achieving a new unity is a deeper sensitivity to the "pilgrim" nature of the church.[14] A church which feels that it has "arrived" and is always looking back tends to accumulate a heavy load of institutional luggage. A Christian community which is constantly moving forward must travel more lightly. It must not be encumbered with excessive paraphernalia. It must know the difference between the equipment strictly essential to its pilgrimage and that which is dispensable for the march ahead.

We must all admit that as of today we are not spiritually prepared for "one great church." Before there can be meaningful union in the organizational realm, there are prior conditions that we must meet in the realm of the spirit. We must learn to love not only other Christians but also the churches of other Christians—a much more difficult thing. Not until Presbyterians like

[13] *The Emergence of a World Christian Community* (New Haven: Yale University Press, 1949), pp. 54–55.

[14] I owe my appreciation of the phrase to the address by the German theologian, Professor Edmund Schlink, at the Lund Conference on Faith and Order.

myself have really come to appreciate the Christian insights and cherish the Christian witness of Anglican, Lutheran, Methodist, Baptist, and still other churches, will corporate union with them have any creative significance.

We must all come also to a clearer discernment of the partial and relative nature of the truth which each historic group of Christians possesses, and consequently to a greater passion for the wholeness of the church. Without that, each of us will go on assuming that he already enjoys the full richness of the Christian heritage, not realizing that it is only in company "with all the saints" that we can "comprehend what is the breadth and height and depth" of the love of Christ mediated to us through His Church.

Finally, we must be more aware that unity in the church depends upon a deepened sense of mission to the world. Churches that are self-centered in their interests and concerned with their institutional prestige will never make a great advance toward unity. If we are to have a Church united we must have a church reborn. It is in proportion as all the churches lose their pride in present status, confess how gravely they are failing to be a worthy channel of our Lord's purpose, and dedicate themselves to Him anew, that we can hope for the answer to His prayer "that they all may be one."

THE WILLIAM HENRY HOOVER
LECTURESHIP ON CHRISTIAN UNITY

The Disciples Divinity House of the
University of Chicago

The William Henry Hoover Lectureship on Christian Unity was established by the Disciples Divinity House at the University of Chicago in 1945. Resources for the Lectureship are a trust Fund established in the amount of fifty thousand dollars some years prior to his death by Mr. William Henry Hoover, of North Canton, Ohio. The purpose of the Fund was designated as the promotion of Christian unity, a cause for which Mr. Hoover demonstrated a lifelong interest. It was decided that the cause could best be served by establishing at a major university center a lectureship on Christian unity, no such lectureship having yet come into existence. The Disciples Divinity House of the University of Chicago was asked to accept Mr. Hoover's Trust for the purposes of sponsoring a lectureship on Christian unity.

The intention of those establishing the Lectureship is that each lecturer shall be a distinguished Christian churchman, whose experience, research and knowledge eminently qualify him to discuss the problem of Christian unity and to make a positive contribution toward closer co-operation of the many Christian denominations and the ultimate unity of the church of Christ.

A series of lectures is normally to be given annually and to be published as the Hoover Lectures.

Chapters I, II, VII, and VIII of the present book were originally delivered in a somewhat briefer form as the Hoover Lectures for 1958.

SELECTED BIBLIOGRAPHY

This reading list is not designed to give a complete bibliography for the specialized student. It is deliberately selective. It includes the publications to which I am most indebted or which I regard as most likely to be helpful for supplementary reading. I omit many important titles which are available only in French and German. I give special attention to publications which have appeared since 1950 and which are therefore not covered by earlier bibliographies.

The titles are arranged in eight sections corresponding to the themes of the eight chapters of this book, preceded by a general section suggesting background material for an understanding of the ecumenical movement as a whole.

More exhaustive listings may be found in the following bibliographies:

Senaud, A., *Christian Unity: A Bibliography*. Geneva: World's Committee of Y.M.C.A.'s, 1937. Nearly 2,000 titles, including many in French and German, from the middle of the nineteenth century to 1937.

Brandreth, H. R. T., *Unity and Reunion: A Bibliography* (2nd ed.). London: Adam and Charles Black, 1948. About 1,200 titles, with special concern for publications in the field of Faith and Order or having to do with concrete efforts for union.

Macy, Paul G., *An Ecumenical Bibliography*. An appendix of twenty-two pages to William Adams Brown's *Toward a United Church*. New York: Charles Scribner's Sons, 1946.

Rouse, Ruth, and Neill, Stephen C. An appendix to *A History of the Ecumenical Movement, 1517–1948*. Philadelphia: Westminster Press, 1954. Forty pages of references, comprehensive and carefully classified, including both general background and developments between 1910 and 1948.

For resources of information such as are found in annual reports, unpublished documents, and other archives, the following libraries have valuable collections:

William Adams Brown Ecumenical Library, Union Theological Seminary, New York, N. Y.

Missionary Research Library, Union Theological Seminary, New York, N. Y.

Day Historical Library of Foreign Missions, Yale Divinity School, New Haven, Conn.

Library of the World Council of Churches, Geneva, Switzerland.

Library of the National Council of the Churches of Christ in the U.S.A., Interchurch Center, New York, N. Y.

GENERAL BACKGROUND

Bell, G. K. A. (ed.). *Documents on Christian Unity*, four series. London: Oxford University Press, 1924, 1930, 1948, 1957.

Bergendoff, Conrad. *The One Holy Catholic Apostolic Church*. Rock Island, Ill.: Augustana Press, 1954.

Bilheimer, Robert S. *The Quest for Christian Unity*. New York: Association Press, 1952.

Bingle, E. J., and Grubb, Kenneth. *World Christian Handbook*. London: World Dominion Press, 1957.

Brauer, Jerald C. *Protestantism in America*. Philadelphia: Westminster Press, 1953.

Brown, William Adams. *The Church, Catholic and Protestant: A Study of Differences that Matter*. New York: Charles Scribner's Sons, 1956.

Cavert, Samuel McCrea, and Van Dusen, Henry P. (eds.). *The Church through Half a Century*. New York: Charles Scribner's Sons, 1936.

Committee on the War and the Religious Outlook. *Christian Unity: Its Principles and Possibilities*. New York: Association Press, 1921.

Dun, Angus. *The Meaning of Unity*. New York: Harper & Brothers, 1937.

Flew, R. Newton (ed.). *The Nature of the Church: Papers Presented to the Theological Commission of the World Conference on Faith and Order*. New York: Harper & Brothers, 1952.

Handy, Robert T. *We Witness Together: A History of Cooperative Home Missions*. New York: Friendship Press, 1956.

Horton, Walter M. *Christian Theology: An Ecumenical Approach* (rev. ed.). New York: Harper & Brothers, 1958.

Latourette, Kenneth S. *A History of Christianity*. New York: Harper & Brothers, 1953.

————. *The Emergence of a World Christian Community*. New Haven: Yale University Press, 1949.

Marty, Martin E. *A Short History of Christianity*. New York: Meridian Books, 1959.

McNeill, John T. *Unitive Protestantism*. Nashville: Abingdon Press, 1930.

Molland, Einar. *Christendom: The Christian Churches, Their Doctrines, Constitutional Forms and Ways of Worship* (trans. from the Norwegian). London: Mowbridge, 1959.

Muelder, Walter G. *Foundations of the Responsible Society*. Nashville: Abingdon Press, 1959.

Nelson, J. Robert. *The Realm of Redemption: Studies in the Doctrine of the Nature of the Church in Contemporary Protestant Theology*. Chicago: Wilcox and Follett, 1951.

Newbigin, Lesslie. *The Household of God*. New York: Friendship Press, 1953.

Niebuhr, H. Richard. *The Social Sources of Denominationalism*. New York: Henry Holt and Company, 1929.

Ramsey, Arthur Michael. *An Era in Anglican Theology: From Gore to Temple*. New York: Charles Scribner's Sons, 1960.

Rouse, Ruth, and Neill, Stephen C. (eds.). *A History of the Ecumenical Movement: 1517–1948*. Philadelphia: Westminster Press, 1954.

Slosser, Gaius Jackson. *Christian Unity*. New York: E. P. Dutton, 1929.

Söderblom, Nathan. *Christian Fellowship*. New York: Fleming H. Revell, 1923.

Spinka, Matthew. *The Quest for Church Unity*. New York: The Macmillan Company, 1960.

Van Dusen, Henry P. *World Christianity*. Nashville: Abingdon Press, 1947.

Visser 't Hooft, W. A. *The Renewal of the Church*. Philadelphia: Westminster Press, 1956.

Visser 't Hooft, W. A., and Oldham, J. H. *The Church and Its Function in Society*. New York: Harper & Brothers, 1937.

CHAPTER I.   THE ROAD WE HAVE TRAVELED
Survey of a Half Century

Bate, H. N. (ed.). *Faith and Order: Proceedings of the World Conference, Lausanne, August 3–21, 1927*. New York: George H. Doran Company, 1927.

Bell, G. K. A. (ed.). *The Stockholm Conference, 1925*. London: Oxford University Press, 1926.

Brown, William Adams. *Toward a United Church: Three Decades of Ecumenical Christianity*. New York: Charles Scribner's Sons, 1946.

Carter, Paul A. *The Decline and Revival of the Social Gospel, 1920–1940*. Ithaca: Cornell University Press, 1954.

Gairdner, W. H. T. *Echoes from Edinburgh, 1910*. New York: Fleming H. Revell, 1910.

Goodall, Norman. *The Ecumenical Movement: What It is and Does*. London and New York: Oxford University Press, 1961.

Hodgson, Leonard (ed.). *Second World Conference on Faith and Order, Edinburgh, 1937*. London: SCM Press, 1937.

Hogg, W. Richey. *Ecumenical Foundations: A History of the International Missionary Council and Its Nineteenth-Century Background*. New York: Harper & Brothers, 1952.

Horton, Walter M. *Toward a Reborn Church*. New York: Harper & Brothers, 1949.

Jurji, Edward J. (ed.). *The Ecumenical Era in Church and Society*. New York: The Macmillan Company, 1959.

Lee, Robert. *The Social Sources of Church Unity*. Nashville: Abingdon Press, 1960.

Macfarland, Charles S. *Christian Unity in Practice and Prophecy*. New York: The Macmillan Company, 1933.

Macy, Paul G. *If It Be of God: The Story of the World Council of Churches*. St. Louis: Bethany Press, 1960.

Miller Robert Moats. *American Protestantism and Social Ideals: 1919–1939*. Chapel Hill: University of North Carolina Press, 1958.

Minear, Paul S. (ed.). *The Nature of the Unity We Seek*. Official Report of the North American Conference on Faith and Order, Oberlin, O., 1957; St. Louis: Bethany Press, 1958.

Neill, Stephen C. *Brothers of the Faith: The Story of Men Who Have Worked for Christian Unity*. Nashville: Abingdon Press, 1960.

Oldham, J. H. (ed.). *The Oxford Conference: Official Report*. New York: Harper & Brothers, 1937.

Rouse, Ruth, and Neill, Stephen C. *A History of the Ecumenical Movement: 1517–1948*. Philadelphia: Westminster Press, 1954, chaps. 8–16.

Tomkins, Oliver S. (ed.). *The Third World Conference on Faith and Order, Lund, 1952*. London: SCM Press, 1953.

Visser 't Hooft, W. A. (ed.). *The First Assembly of the World Council of Churches, Amsterdam, 1948*. New York: Harper & Brothers, 1949.

———. (ed.). *The Evanston Report: Second Assembly of the World Council of Churches*. New York: Harper & Brothers, 1955.

CHAPTER II.   THE CROSSROADS WHERE WE ARE
Survey of the Present Scene

Bell, G. K. A. *The Kingship of Christ*. Harmondsworth, England: Penguin Books, 1954.

Chandler, Edgar H. S. *The High Tower of Refuge: The Work of the World Council for Refugees*. London: Odhams Press, 1959.

Cooke, Leslie E. *The Church Is There: An Interpretation of the Program of Interchurch Aid*. Greenwich, Conn.: Seabury House, 1957.

Duff, Edward, S.J. *The Social Thought of the World Council of Churches*. New York: Association Press, 1956.

Ecumenical Review, The. A Quarterly published by the World Council of Churches, Geneva, 1948–.

Ecumenical Press Service. Mimeographed Weekly Bulletin of Information, published by World Council of Churches, Geneva.

Minutes of the Annual Meetings of the Central Committee of the World Council of Churches. Geneva, 1949–.

CHAPTER III.   FELLOW PILGRIMS ON THE ROAD
Asian and African Churches in the Ecumenical Movement

A Decisive Hour for the Christian Mission. Addresses by Norman Goodall, Lesslie Newbigin, W. A. Visser 't Hooft, D. T. Niles. London: SCM Press, 1960.

Bouquet, A. C. *The Christian Faith and Non-Christian Religions*. New York: Harper & Brothers, 1958.

Bridston, Keith. *Shock and Renewal: The Christian Mission Enters a New Era*. New York: Friendship Press, 1955.

Devanandan, Paul. "The Religious and Spiritual Climate of India Today," *Ecumenical Review*, April, 1956. Geneva: World Council of Churches.

Hogg, W. Richey. *One World, One Mission*. New York: Friendship Press, 1960.

International Review of Missions, The. Quarterly Journal of the International Missionary Council. London, 1912—.

Kraemer, Hendrik. *World Cultures and World Religions*. Philadelphia: Westminster Press, 1961.

Latourette, Kenneth S. *A History of the Expansion of Christianity* (Vols. VI and VII). New York: Harper & Brothers, 1937–1945.

Manikam, Rajah B. *Christianity and the Asian Revolution*. New York: Friendship Press, 1955.

Newbigin, Lesslie. *One Body, One Gospel, One World*. New York: International Missionary Council, 1958.

Neill, Stephen C. *The Unfinished Task*. London: Lutterworth Press, 1957.

Perry, Edmund. *The Gospel in Dispute: The Relation of the Christian Faith to Other Missionary Religions*. Garden City, N. Y.: Doubleday and Company, 1958.

Warren, Max. *Challenge and Response*. New York: Morehouse-Barlow, 1959.

Webster, Douglas. "The Foreign Missionary Today," *Theology Today*, January, 1960 (Vol. XVI: No. 4).

CHAPTER IV.   MORE FELLOW PILGRIMS ON THE ROAD
Eastern Orthodox in the Ecumenical Movement

Brown, William Adams. *The Church, Catholic and Protestant*. New York: Charles Scribner's Sons, 1935, chaps. 6, 8, 14.

Bulgakov, S. *The Orthodox Church*. London: Centenary Press, 1935.

Christian East, The. Quarterly Organ of the Anglican and Eastern Churches Association, London, 1920—.

Fedotov, G. P. (ed.). *A Treasury of Russian Spirituality*. New York: Sheed and Ward, 1950.

Florovsky, Georges. "One Holy Catholic Apostolic Church," *The Universal Church in God's Design* (Amsterdam Assembly Series, Vol. I), New York: Harper & Brothers, 1948, pp. 59–67.

Gavin, Frank. *Some Aspects of Contemporary Greek Orthodox Thought*. Milwaukee: Morehouse Company, 1923.

Hammond, Peter. *The Waters of Marah: The Present State of the Greek Church*. New York: The Macmillan Company, 1956.

Schlink, Edmund. "The Significance of the Eastern and Western Traditions for the Christian Church," *Ecumenical Review*, January, 1960 (Vol. XII: No. 2).

Sobornost. Quarterly Journal of the Fellowship of St. Alban and St. Sergius, London, 1935–.

Zankov, Stefan. *The Eastern Orthodox Church*. Milwaukee: Morehouse Company, 1929.

Zernov, Nicolas. *The Church of the Eastern Christians*. London: SPCK Press, 1942.

———. *The Russians and Their Church*. London: SPCK Press, 1954.

———. "The Eastern Schism and the Eastern Orthodox Church," *The Concise Encyclopedia of Living Faiths* (R. C. Zaehner, ed.), New York: Hawthorne Books, 1959, pp. 86–107.

CHAPTER V. ROADS THAT DIVERGE
Non-co-operating Protestants and the Ecumenical Movement

Christianity Today: A Fortnightly Journal. Washington, D. C.: 1956–.

Colquhoun, Frank. *The Fellowship of the Gospel*. London: Evangelical Alliance, 1955.

Franzmann, Martin H. "The Nature of the Unity We Seek: A Missouri Synod Lutheran View," *Religion in Life*, Spring, 1957 (Vol. XXVI: No. 2).

Goodall, Norman. "Evangelicals and Evangelicals," *Frontier:* A Quarterly. London: October, 1958 (Vol. I: No. 4).

Kik, J. Marcellus. *Ecumenism and the Evangelical*. Philadelphia: Presbyterian and Reformed Publishing Society, 1958.

Lee, Robert. *The Social Sources of Church Unity*. Nashville: Abingdon Press, 1960, chap. 8.

Murch, James De Forest. *Co-operation without Compromise: A His-*

tory of the National Association of Evangelicals. Grand Rapids: Eerdmans Publishing Co., 1956.

Newbigin, Lesslie. *The Household of God*. New York: Friendship Press, 1953, chaps. 1–4.

Paulk, E. P. *Your Pentecostal Neighbor*. Cleveland, Tenn.: Pathway Press, 1958.

Price, Theron D. "The Nature of the Unity We Seek: A Southern Baptist View," *Religion in Life*, Spring, 1957 (Vol. XXVI: No. 2).

Roy, Ralph Lord. *Apostles of Discord*. Boston: Beacon Press, 1953, chaps. 8–10.

Van Dusen, Henry P. *Spirit, Son and Father*. New York: Charles Scribner's Sons, 1958, chaps. 4, 8.

Chapter VI.   MORE ROADS THAT DIVERGE
Roman Catholics and the Ecumenical Movement

Brown, Robert McAfee, and Weigel, Gustave, S.J. *An American Dialogue: A Protestant Looks at Catholicism and a Catholic Looks at Protestantism*. New York: Sheed and Ward, 1960.

A. Protestant Writings:

Bates, M. Searle. *Religious Liberty: An Inquiry*. New York: International Missionary Council, 1945.

Bennett, John C. *Christians and the State*. New York: Charles Scribner's Sons, 1958, chap. 17.

Brown, Robert McAfee. *The Spirit of Protestantism*. New York: Oxford University Press, 1961.

Carillo de Albornoz, A. F. *Roman Catholicism and Religious Liberty*. Geneva: World Council of Churches, 1959.

Hudson, Winthrop S. *Understanding Roman Catholicism*. Philadelphia: Westminster Press, 1959.

Koenker, Ernest B. *The Liturgical Renaissance in the Roman Catholic Church*. Chicago: University of Chicago Press, 1954.

Pelikan, Jaroslav. *The Riddle of Roman Catholicism*. Nashville: Abingdon Press, 1959.

Skydsgaard, K. E. *One in Christ*. Trans. A. C. Kildegaard, Philadelphia: Muhlenberg Press, 1957.

———. "The Roman Catholic Church and the Ecumenical Movement," *The Universal Church in God's Design* (Amsterdam Assembly Series, Vol. I). New York: Harper & Brothers, 1948.

Tillich, Paul. *The Protestant Era.* Chicago: University of Chicago Press, 1948.

Underwood, Kenneth. *Protestant and Catholic.* Boston: Beacon Press, 1957.

B. ROMAN CATHOLIC WRITINGS:

Adam, Karl. *The Spirit of Catholicism.* Garden City, N. Y.: Doubleday and Company, 1954.

————. *One and Holy.* Trans. Cecily Hastings. New York: Sheed and Ward, 1951.

Bouyer, Charles, S.J. *The Spirit and Forms of Protestantism.* Trans. A. V. Littledale. Westminster, Md.: Newman Press, 1956.

Congar, Yves. *Divided Christendom.* Trans. M. A. Bousfield. London: Geoffrey Bles, 1939.

Dumont, C. J., O.P. (ed.). *Approaches to Christian Unity.* Trans. Henry St. John, O.P. Baltimore: Helicon Press, 1959.

Lemming, Bernard, S.J. *The Church and the Churches: A Study of Ecumenism.* London: Darton, Longman and Todd, 1960.

Mehl, Roger. "The Ecclesiological Significance of the World Council from a Roman Catholic Standpoint," *Ecumenical Review,* April, 1957.

Murray, John Courtney, S.J. *We Hold These Truths.* New York: Sheed and Ward, 1960.

Tavard, George H. *The Catholic Approach to Protestantism.* New York: Harper & Brothers, 1955.

————. *Holy Writ or Holy Church.* New York: Harper & Brothers, 1960.

Todd, John M. *Catholicism and the Ecumenical Movement.* London: Longmans, Green and Company, 1956.

Weigel, Gustave, S.J. *A Catholic Primer on the Ecumenical Movement.* Westminster, Md.: Newman Press, 1957.

CHAPTER VII. THE ROAD AHEAD
Where Local and Ecumenical Meet

Douglass, H. Paul. *Protestant Co-operation in American Cities.* New York: Institute of Social and Religious Research, 1930.

Douglass, Truman B. *Preaching and the New Reformation.* New York: Harper & Brothers, 1956.

Kean, Charles D. "Christian Unity in the Local Congregation," *Religion in Life,* Spring, 1957 (Vol. XXVI: No. 2).

Miller, J. Quinter. *Growing Together: A Manual for Councils of Churches.* New York: National Council of the Churches of Christ in the U.S.A., 1955.

———. *Christian Unity: Its Relevance to the Community.* Shenandoah, Va.: Shenandoah Publishing House, 1957.

Neill, Stephen C. "Christian Unity at the Local Level," *Religion in Life,* Spring, 1957 (Vol. XXVI, No. 2).

Sanderson, Ross W. *The Nation-Wide Background and Ecumenical Significance of State and Local Councils of Churches.* New York: Association of Councils of Churches, 1960.

Visser 't Hooft, W. A. "The Una Sancta and the Local Church," *Ecumenical Review,* October, 1960 (Vol. XIII: No. 1).

CHAPTER VIII. THE FAR HORIZON OF THE ROAD
The Goal of the Ecumenical Movement

Bailllie, John, and Marsh, John (eds.). *Intercommunion.* New York: Harper & Brothers, 1952.

Craig, Clarence Tucker. *The One Church in the Light of the New Testament.* Nashville: Abingdon Press, 1945.

Douglass, H. Paul. *Church Unity Movements in the United States.* New York: Institute of Social and Religious Research, 1934.

———. *A Decade of Objective Progress in Church Unity, 1927–1936.* Report to Edinburgh Conference on Faith and Order. New York: Harper & Brothers, 1937.

Dun, Angus. *Prospecting for a United Church.* New York: Harper & Brothers, 1948.

Garrison, Winfred E. *The Quest and Character of a United Church.* Nashville: Abingdon Press, 1957.

Kean, Charles Duell. *The Road to Reunion.* Greenwich, Conn.: Seabury Press, 1958.

Kirk, Kenneth E. (ed.). *The Apostolic Ministry.* London: Hodder and Stoughton, 1946.

Knox, John. *The Early Church and the Coming Great Church.* Nashville: Abingdon Press, 1955.

Legg, A. H. "The Unity of the Church," *Ecumenical Review*, July, 1960 (Vol. XII: No. 4).

Manson, T. W. *The Church's Ministry*. Philadelphia: Westminster Press, 1948.

Minear, Paul S. (ed.). *The Nature of the Unity We Seek: Official Report of the North American Conference on Faith and Order, 1957*. St. Louis: Bethany Press, 1958.

Morrison, C. C. *The Unfinished Reformation*. New York, Harper & Brothers, 1953.

Negotiating Committee for Church Union in North India and Pakistan, Plan of Church Union (3rd ed.). Madras: Christian Literature Society, 1957.

Neill, Stephen C. *Towards Church Union, 1937–1952: A Survey of Approaches to Closer Union*. Geneva: Faith and Order Commission, 1952.

Newbigin, Lesslie. *The Reunion of the Church: A Defense of the South India Scheme*. New York: Harper & Brothers, 1948.

———. *The Household of God*. New York: Friendship Press, 1954.

Outler, Albert C. *The Christian Tradition and the Unity We Seek*. New York: Oxford University Press, 1957.

Pittenger, W. Norman. *The Church, the Ministry and Reunion*. Greenwich, Conn.: Seabury Press, 1957.

Richardson, Cyril C. *The Sacrament of Reunion*. New York: Charles Scribner's Sons, 1940.

Silcox, Claris E. *Church Union in Canada*. New York: Institute of Social and Religious Research, 1933.

Sundkler, B. G. M. *The Church of South India: The Movement towards Union, 1900–1947*. London: Lutterworth Press, 1954.

Tomkins, Oliver S. *The Wholeness of the Church*. London: SCM Press, 1949.

Universal Church in God's Design, The. (Amsterdam Series, Vol. I). New York: Harper & Brothers, 1948.

Visser 't Hooft, W. A. *The Pressure of Our Common Calling*. Garden City, N. Y.: Doubleday and Company, 1959.

Wedel, T. O. *The Coming Great Church*. New York: The Macmillan Company, 1945.

Ways of Worship: Report of a Theological Commission of Faith and Order. New York: Harper & Brothers, 1951.

INDEX